Hubert d'Ornano

Boundless beauty

Conception and Edition:
Félix Torres

Graphic design:
Pierre-Olivier Leroy
L.C Création
Tel. (+33) 6 60 67 81 57

Production: Ex Fabrica
www.exfabrica.fr
Printing: Grafiche Flaminia, Trevi (Italy).

FÉLIX TORRES ÉDITEUR
23, rue du Cherche-Midi 75006 PARIS FRANCE
51, rue du Maréchal de Lattre de Tassigny 91450 SOISY-SUR-SEINE
Tel. (+33) 1 60 75 85 61 Mob. (+33) 6 15 05 44 43
Email: contact@felix-torres-editeur.com
www.felix-torres-editeur.com

ISBN: 978-2-912348-20-3

You can consult our catalogue for the latest news and information on our upcoming publications on our site www.felix-torres-editeur.com

Hubert d'Ornano

Boundless beauty

FÉLIX TORRES ÉDITEUR

970s, with Isabelle and our children; Philippe, Marc, Élisabeth, Laetitia and Christine

Table of Contents

Foreword

This is a story of the d'Ornano family, which is also the story of Sisley. The d'Ornanos are a Corsican family that has produced three Maréchaux de France and a French Cabinet Minister.

It is the story of a remarkable Polish ancestry, the country where I was born in 1926, and of the three Polish figures closely connected to my family: Marie Walewska, Elisabeth d'Ornano née Michalska and Isabelle d'Ornano née Potocka.

It tells of our family's first steps in the world of cosmetics, when my father Guillaume d'Ornano co-founded his first skincare brand in the 1930s. After the Second World War, he joined my brother Michel and me in a perfume and skincare venture he had helped us to start some years earlier. With the help of my wife Isabelle, and, later on, of my children, we have developed it to be the global success it is today, whilst expressing the spirit of the family, the sense of effort and the love of nature.

At my age I now sometimes wonder: "Have I accomplished enough"? That is why I am writing these personal memoirs which might interest my descendants, those who have worked, work now, and will work for Sisley as well as those who use and enjoy our products. This story also reflects the values, ideas, the desire and a sense of style which are those of Sisley, a French skincare company that has become a worldwide brand. I hope this book will help you get to know us better.

Hubert d'Ornano

Chapter 1

A Polish Heart

With my grandmother Alexandra Michalska.

“I was born in a countryside full of green fields, forests and lakes, in Poland. My parents had married in Warsaw five years earlier; I am the fruit of two Franco-Polish loves.”

The marriage of my parents, Guillaume d'Ornano and Elisabeth Michalska, in Warsaw in 1921.

I was born on March 31st 1926 in Melgiew, a castle in the beautiful Polish countryside near the town of Lublin. Poland had recently regained its independence, and in the early 1920s my father, Guillaume d'Ornano, was an attaché at the French Embassy in Warsaw. One day, a charming lady, Alexandra Michalska came to see him for a French visa. So as not to keep her waiting, he suggested she leave her passport and he would drop it off later on, at the Hotel Europejski in the heart of Warsaw where she was staying with her daughter. That evening he met the enchanting Elisabeth. They fell in love at first sight. My father was twenty-six, my mother nineteen. She was already engaged, but promptly gave back a beautiful ruby ring and my parents were married in Warsaw a few months later, on May 21st 1921. It was the second Franco-Polish wedding in the d'Ornano family after the marriage of my great grandfather Philippe-Antoine d'Ornano to Marie Walewska who had been Napoleon's great love. It would not be the last

With my mother Elisabeth and my brother Michel at Trawniki, in the 1930s.

Marie Walewska, Countess d'Ornano

I love saying that I am the fruit of two Franco-Polish loves, a tradition which began a century and a half earlier when my ancestor Philippe-Antoine d'Ornano, then a general and later field marshal of France, married Marie Walewska. Friendship and war always brought the two countries together, and this just added one more link - that of love. Didn't General de Gaulle say in Warsaw in 1967, "The Poles and the French, we are alike in so many ways! "

On January 1st 1807, at the last post house before Warsaw, the Blonie Inn, a beautiful, frail blue-eyed blonde was among those who had come to cheer the Emperor. Like all of Poland they hoped that the conqueror of Austerlitz and Jena, at the height of his power and glory, would free Poland, which was ripped apart and divided between Russia, Prussia and Austria. When she got close to the imperial carriage, she cried out in French,

Philippe-Antoine d'Ornano, who married Marie Walewska on September 7th 1816 in Brussels (painting by Robert Lefèvre).

"Welcome to Poland, My Lord. Save us from the tyrants. The Poles will give their lives for you and you have already captured their hearts!"

Surprised and charmed, Napoleon offered her a bouquet of flowers from his carriage saying, "Keep these as a guarantee of my good intentions - I hope we will meet again in Warsaw!"

The carriage disappeared. Napoleon upon arriving in Warsaw demanded that the young woman be found. Marie was 20 years old and her parents, the Laczynskis, were local aristocrats and lived simply, off the Kiernozia estate. She was the eldest of six children - they were raised by their mother after the death of their father Mathieu Laczynski. She was married off, age seventeen, to Count Anastase Colonna Walewski, a rich seventy-year old neighbour, with whom she had a first child, Antoine.

Marie was a fanatic, an almost mystical patriot, very hostile towards the Russians who occupied a large part of her country. She was quickly found and soon invited to a reception at the Potocki Palace in honour of Napoleon, hosted by Joseph Poniatowski, head of the interim Polish government. She turned the invitation down, but her husband and all of Warsaw pressed her to accept, and she finally gave in. It was whispered to her that she could be God's hand in helping to restore her dear Poland.

Marie Walewska, who died prematurely following the birth of Rodolphe d'Ornano.

The following days Napoleon saw her privately. Their romantic meetings became more frequent and a liaison began which continued after he left Poland. In 1808 he saw her again in Paris and the following year in Austria. In 1810 Marie gave birth to Alexandre, Napoleon's son, and she moved with him to Paris.

However, Napoleon had only partially fulfilled the wishes of the Polish patriots. He did not restore their country but only created the Grand Duchy of Warsaw, so as not to anger the Russian Emperor Alexander I.

Marie Walewska and her son Alexandre were at Fontainebleau during the last hours of the Empire, when Napoleon abdicated. They even visited him on the Island of Elba– but their liaison belonged to the past. She saw him one last time at La Malmaison after his defeat at Waterloo.

From 1812 Marie met frequently with the young Colonel of the

> Philippe-Antoine wrote to Marie on May 2nd 1813:
>
> –"Please accept my deepest gratitude for welcoming me with such charming grace and giving me your time– the feelings you inspire in me make me even more indebted to you. Even if they were never shared they have given me many hours of great happiness of which it seems forbidden to ask more. I shall wait. Philippe-Antoine."
>
> Marie replies on June 20th: "I also have very fond memories of those weeks. They sealed our friendship– It is to them that I owe your kind letter and it gives me pleasure to write you."

Dragoons, Philippe-Antoine d'Ornano, whom she had first met in Warsaw in July, 1807. However, although Marie was since divorced from her husband, Count Walewski, she did not consider herself free to re-marry whilst he was still alive. When Philippe-Antoine returned to Germany they wrote to each other.

Philippe-Antoine was commander of the Horse Guards in charge of defending Paris and saw Marie every day. When the Bourbons returned, he again insisted to marry her. With the ultimate obstacles to their union removed– her husband's death and the collapse of the Empire, they were engaged in February 1815. They married a year later, on September 7th 1816, at the Collegiate Saint-Michel-et-Gudule in

"Marie Walewska left an exceptional mark in the history of France and Poland. She forever symbolises the perpetual and sensual relationship which unites the two countries."

Brussels. Philippe-Antoine, who joined Napoleon during the final Hundred Days, was in fact banished by the Bourbons in France. Nine months after their marriage, on June 9th 1817, Marie gave birth to her third child Rodolphe-Auguste. She would not recover, suffering from puerperal fever complicated by nephritis. She managed to return to her country one last time in January. On a cold, wet and snowy day in Paris on December 11th 1817, she died surrounded by her husband and her three sons. She was thirty-one years old.

Alexandre Walewski, Napoleon's son, later said that the entire household was overwhelmed with sorrow. "General d'Ornano's grief was beyond imagination: My Mother was one of the most remarkable women who had ever lived."

Napoleon's son went on to have a brilliant career. Four times Ambassador, President of the National Assembly after the death of the Duc de Morny, he became the French Foreign Minister, under the reign of Napoleon III. Philippe-Antoine never remarried and survived forty-six years after Marie's death. He kept her heart in an urn with the inscription "Marie Laczynski, Countess d'Ornano [...]". It lies today in the d'Ornano vault in the Père Lachaise cemetery. Just before her death, my great-grandmother said: "If my heart is in Paris, my body will be in Poland". So a few months after her death, according to her wishes, her body was transferred to her native country and is buried in the Kiernozia family vault.

Napoleon and Marie Walewska, painting by Claudius Berr.

As a woman, Marie Walewska left France and Poland a unique legacy. Her name will forever be a symbol of the strong relationship between France and Poland. If Marie had two great loves in her lifetime –Napoleon and Philippe-Antoine– she loved her two countries with equal passion, her native Poland, and her beloved adopted country, France. When I married Isabelle Potocka, herself Polish, I added a new link to the chain. Perhaps one of my grandchildren or great-grandchildren will do the same? Who knows?

A Polish childhood

My father, Guillaume d'Ornano, was born in Tours on the banks of the Loire River on June 25th 1894. After fighting in World War I, by the end of which he had attained the rank of Captain, he began a diplomatic career, just like his grandfather, Rodolphe d'Ornano, the son of Philippe-Antoine and Marie, and his great-uncle, Alexander Walewski. Rodolphe d'Ornano was an attaché at the French legation in Dresden, and later at the French Embassy in London; but as a fervent supporter of Napoleon III, actively backing his return to power and to the throne, he had to abandon this career. Napoleon III appointed him Chamberlain, master of ceremonies of the Court and Commander of the Legion of Honour.

My father arrived in Warsaw in the early 1920s. Poland was still a very young country, newly reborn in 1918 following the divisions in 1772, 1793 and 1795 which had led to its disappearance from the map of Europe. My parents left for France two years later. My brother Michel was born in Paris in July 1924, but my mother chose to return to her native country to give birth to her second child as my father was in the throes of a political campaign. I spent the first eight years of my life in Trawniki, my grandmother's property. My mother's mother, Alexandra Michalska, ran the property alone. Her husband, my grandfather, had died at an early age– I never got to know him.

Alexandra Michalska was a real character! Believing beyond any doubt that the air of new Poland was best for me, she almost "kidnapped" me twice. The first time was just after I was born, as she kept me at home with her for several years. The second time was when, at the age of seven, I returned to France, rather unhappy. My parents had rented a house in Cabourg in Normandy for the holidays. My grandmother came with us and one day she said to my father: "Well, we are going shopping to buy Hubert what he needs for school."

The château of Melgiew, where I was born in 1926, my aunt Rulikowska's home.

At my cousins' in Suchodoly, in the 1930s.

In the car with my mother Elisabeth.

Without anyone knowing, we immediately boarded a train, via Paris and Gare de l'Est, bound for Poland! When my father realised what had happened, he picked up the telephone and called his friend, the Paris Police Commissioner, Jean Chiappe, who also happened to be Corsican. But it was too late; the train was already in Germany, it was impossible to stop it... and so I spent an extra year in Poland. Polish women, especially those of my family, are truly unbelievable!

I grew up in the Polish highlands "Malopolska" –Little Poland– the historic heart of the country, between Warsaw and Krakow, the former capital. A flat peaceful landscape along the banks of the Wieprz River, a beautiful countryside of fields and forests, dotted with tiny villages, mansions, wooden churches and wild rivers flowing down from the mountains in the South. We lived at Trawniki a vast fertile estate of several thousand hectares producing large quantities of wheat, beet and wood, which was expertly run by my grandmother, despite her widowhood. In the summer, from my bedroom window I could watch the huge loads of wood being transported from the Tatra mountains down the Wieprz that flowed past the family property heading to the Vistula and the Baltic Sea.

> "*We are almost already in that famous part of Poland 'the fringes', the* kresy *in Polish, rolling imperceptibly towards the wide open spaces of Eastern Europe, this immense borderless plain which stretches to the Urals.*"

I learned to swim in the river's wild, rapid waters. We were almost at the edge of the *kresy*, the Borderlands of Poland, rolling imperceptibly towards the wide open spaces of Eastern Europe, this immense borderless plain which stretches to the Urals. The family of Isabelle, my wife, owned large properties in these endless spaces between Poland, Lithuania, Belarus, Russia and Ukraine, some of which became inaccessible after the Great War following the arbitrary delineation of new borders, particularly between Poland and Ukraine.

Trawniki was in no way a sleepy, backward medieval citadel. At the time it was a modern estate, a small community where hundreds of people worked, with a series of horse-drawn rail wagons running

Nearly an adolescent in the fields at Trawniki. The war would soon make my maternal family's Polish universe disappear.

through the property. In winter when everything was covered with snow, we used sleighs to get around, but with spring the roads became a sea of mud and were often impassable. My aunt, my mother's sister, Countess Komorowska, lived in nearby Lublin and we often visited her. I used to stuff myself with "*pierogi*" –the delicious Polish ravioli– I once managed to eat forty and was nicknamed "the forty *pierogi* martyr"!

Everyone had their place in this world, just like in the Polish-Jewish community. Wearing frocks and caps, they ensured trade, a sign of confidence. We sold them our wheat at a fair price, and they ensured the payment of the harvest, an assurance of reliability that was renewed mutually the following year. The communities were complementary but differed in their religion and the way they dressed. They coexisted but did not mix.

I played in the woods every day, ran, rode and got into fights, was given a gun at an early age and was taught to shoot by my uncle.

I grew up in great freedom, playing with the children of the farmers who were my age and we all looked alike. Everyone knew and respected each other. All problems went back to my grandmother whose authority was unquestioned. "Don't go into detail, just find a solution", we would hear her say to her agent Mr Soudorowski, who lived and had his office on the ground floor of the palace. My grandmother was highly respected but could be formidable: we sometimes saw her with her cane in the air running after one of us! Her bed was her office– every morning, lying in it she would give her instructions to her staff who were standing behind the door, on the landing!

"I grew up in the highlands, what we call over there 'Malopolska', the 'little Poland', the historical heart of the country between Warsaw and Krakow. A flat, peaceful landscape on the edge of the Wieprz river, one of the tributaries of the Vistula."

Titles are not usually used in Poland, but her coat of arms was displayed above the entrance, as was the custom there. My grandmother's authority resided primarily in the leadership and moral cohesion of the community. She was consulted to enrol a child in school, a son in the army, give someone a job or boost a career, endorse a wedding, attend a christening... A little state within the state governed by patronage, solidarity and interpersonal relationships forged over the generations. The family was highly regarded, considered extremely honest with a sense of justice, and very hard working: laziness in any form was not tolerated.

We prayed before every meal, and we never missed Sunday Mass in the neighbouring village of Biskupice. Catholicism is engraved in the heart of every Pole; it is the singular expression of the soul of the nation and the deep faith that inspires it. Every Sunday we sang the national anthem, Dabrowski's mazurka composed in 1797; the lyrics are beautiful and powerful: "Poland has not yet perished, as long as we live, what foreign violence has seized, with sabres in hand we shall retrieve".

A few birds…

The new Poland where I grew up, one of the oldest nations in Europe, had not existed for 125 years as it had been carved up among its three neighbours, Russia, Prussia and Austria. The fate of several members of my wife Isabelle's family, the Potockis, was proof of this over and over again. Her grandfather, Joseph Potocki, sat on the Saint Petersburg Duma in 1910, which reformed the Russian empire. Her maternal great grandfather, Ferdinand Radziwill, was a member of the Bundestag in Berlin. Her father's grandfather, Alfred Potocki, was even a Prime Minister of the Emperor Francis Joseph in Vienna, a mark of exceptional trust, but also of the Austro-Hungarian domination which gave considerable autonomy to the area of Poland it administered and left an impressive legacy thanks to the quality of its administration and public facilities.

Poland regained independence in 1919, but was fragile, cut out of territories which were for a long time one and the same. Despite the efforts of Isabelle's grandfather, Joseph Potocki, the treaty of Versailles deprived him of his property, several tens of thousands of hectares. It remained but about two kilometres on the other side of the new border with Ukraine. A battle with Soviet Russia at the gates of Warsaw had just ended in victory for the new Polish army. The "Miracle on the Vistula" as it was also known, pushed the onslaught of the Bolsheviks further east. A promising young French officer, Charles de Gaulle, who also fought in the battle, told a friend "major disasters lie ahead". In 1939, the fourth division of Poland between Hitler's Germany and the USSR, the Nazi occupation, and the war between these two totalitarian giants plunged the country into one of its darkest periods in history. Millions of Poles perished and the Holocaust almost destroyed the country's entire Jewish community. Poland, devastated, completely remodelled and moved several hundred kilometres further west, found itself for many years on the other side of the Iron Curtain.

After my “kidnapping”, my father was concerned about my education so he sent “Mademoiselle” to Trawniki. In despair Mademoiselle wrote several distraught letters back to my father:
“I would be more useful if I could actually see your son. He spends all day in the stables or running around barefoot. You’d better come and get him before it is too late.” And so my Polish childhood came to an end.

There would be no third abduction! I returned to France for good in 1934. My brother Michel and I did return to Poland each summer, however; he stayed in Glowno with our Aunt Komorowska, and I in Trawniki. My last stay was in the summer just before the Second World War broke out. I was thirteen and my grandmother said the day before we left:
“Go shooting and bring back a few birds.”

“I lived the first years of my life in a society which was still that of Europe before 1914: community, hierarchy, traditions, pride in one’s position, dignity.”

Michel and I took the last train that left Poland on August 31st 1939. All around us we saw the Polish mobilisation, men cheerfully joining their regiments, while their wives were being comforted. The next day, September 1st at 4.30 am, Hitler’s troops invaded the country where I was born.

The Second World War, followed by Communism led to the demise of Melgiew and Trawniki forever. Aristocratic properties were confiscated or dispersed, the castles, unmaintained, slowly faded from the landscape, and landowners were killed, deported, moved to the cities or emigrated. I spent the first years of my life in a pre-1914 Europe based on community, hierarchy, tradition, pride of rank and dignity. I hope I have inherited some of these values: honour, honesty, respect for others, a certain way of behaving and making decisions– in a word being oneself.

I returned to Poland many times as an adult. The first time was in 1967 with my wife to attend the funeral of her mother’s father, Prince

Janusz Radziwill. When I saw the wonderful green countryside of my childhood again, through the window of the plane, I was so overwhelmed with emotion that the person sitting next to me asked: "Are you OK?"

Thanks to my Polish childhood, I became a citizen of the world, with a much broader view than just the French way of seeing and approaching things. I began my life in one country and I left it for another where I encountered other problems and met other people. I never forgot polish. Isabelle and I speak it, especially when we don't want to be understood! I am at ease everywhere, with anyone, and in any situation.

With Pope Jean-Paul II at Rome in 1985, with Isabelle and our daughter Laetitia at my side.

The Corsican landscape.

Chapter 2

The Ornano name

The Ornano coat of arms from the 16th and 17th centuries.

"We are the descendants of an old Corsican family, the d'Ornanos who, from the 16th to the 20th century, produced three Maréchaux (Marshals) de France, a few French generals and a minister."

We are the descendants of an old Corsican family, the Ornanos. Between the 16th and the 20th century, the family produced three Maréchaux (Marshals) de France, a few French generals and a minister. We descend of Sampiero Corso, a tireless 16th Century Corsican hero who was the first Corsican to offer his services to France. His son, Alphonse, a friend of Catherine de Medici, Charles IX, Henri III and Henri IV, was the first of three d'Ornanos to become a Maréchal de France, followed by his son Jean-Baptiste, and later by one of his descendants, Philippe-Antoine, husband to Marie Walewska and Napoleon's cousin, first Count and general of the Empire– promoted to the rank of Maréchal de France under Napoleon III.

However, at the beginning of the 20th century my grandfather, Alphonse Antoine d'Ornano who was a gambler and played the horses, lost most of his fortune, including his family home during a reckless night. Legend has it that he bet with English bookmakers on his horse winning the Triple Crown (three races in a row)– the 2,000 Guineas Stakes, the Epsom Derby and the St. Leger Stakes. His horse won the first two, but finished second in the third!

Soon after, my grandfather aged only 59, sitting in front of a blazing fireplace, died of a heart attack. It was in 1908, my father was 14 years old. His adolescence, his whole life, his personality would be forever marked by this reversal of fortune and the fall in prestige of his family.

The village of Santa Maria Siché, birthplace of the Ornanos.

From the Medici to the kings of France: Sampiero Corso, the first Corsican hero

Sampiero Corso, first great historic Corsican figure and formidable condottiere, who offered his sword to the service of the Medici, and thereafter the Kings of France.

The d'Ornanos can be traced back as far as the late 13th century to a fiefdom in Ajaccio, southern Corsica. At the beginning of the 15th century the two sons of a Carlo Ornano, Orlando and Alfonso, would create the two future branches of d'Ornanos. The renowned Sampiero de Bastelica, known as Sampiero Corso, with whom our story really begins, stemmed from Alfonso Ornano's side.

Sampiero was born on the island of Corsica at the end of the 15th century, around the towns of Bastelica and Bastelicaccia. A commoner, even though his mother was gentry and a descendant of the Ornano family, he was a young shepherd taking the family herds from the plains to the mountains. However, he would not remain so. In Corsica, his name is as famous as those of Pascal Paoli and Napoleon for being the first to brandish the island's flag against the Republic of Genoa, which was holding the country hostage.

This mighty Corsican legend was undoubtedly a rough individual. He left his impoverished island very early on to make a name for himself on the continent working for the Medici family [1], the great dynasty that ruled Florence and brought it glory. Being involved in many battles, Sampiero quickly distinguished himself by becoming

---

1. This prestigious Florentine family from the Renaissance bestowed two Queens on France, Catherine de Medici, wife to King Henri II and Marie de Medici, wife to King Henri IV.

one of the youngest and most famous condottierre of Italy, which was no mean feat. When the Medici joined the French party, he followed them and in 1533 entered into the service of the kings of France. The first Corsican to go into battle as part of the French army, Sampiero fought in Marignan's victory against the Swiss and in Pavie's defeat against Emperor Charles V. King François I[st] [(2)] made him commander of the ten thousand strong Corsican regiment he created, and in 1527 promoted him to the rank of Colonel General of the Infantry, the highest grade before Maréchal de France. Sampiero Corso was thereafter an integral part in all the sieges and battles. His reputation in combat was such that the Constable of Bourbon said of him:

"In a night of battle, he is worth ten thousand men."

A short time after the death of King François I[st] of France and the accession of his son, Henri II [(3)], Sampiero returned to Corsica to marry Vanina the only daughter of François d'Ornano, an influential nobleman who sided with Genoa in the constant conflicts besetting Corsica. He was forty-five years old, she twenty-three. The marriage was built on the prestige and influence he had acquired as the Colonel of the King of France.

When Sampiero set foot on his native island again, having been imprisoned for a while by the Genoese, who were wary of him, he

2. It is under the reign of this sumptuous, elegant and seductive King of France from 1515 to 1547 that the majority of the chateaux in the Loire, such as Chambord, were built. Although he won the Battle of Marignan (1515), he was defeated and held prisoner by the Emperor Charles Quint at the Battle of Pavie (1525). In the end, he was unable to prevent the conflict between the Catholics and the Protestants to win back his Kingdom.

3. King of France from 1547 to 1559, Henri II was mortally wounded in the eye by the spear of the Captain of the Scottish Guards, Montgomery during a tournament, whilst wearing the favour of Diane de Poitiers, his lifelong 'favourite'. She was the owner of two spectacular chateaux, the Chateau d'Anet as well as the Chateau de Chenonceau in the Loire valley. His premature death left the Kingdom of France, with his sons still minors, under the regency of his wife, Catherine de Medici.

became their mortal enemy. As a champion of the conquest of Corsica on behalf of King Henri II, he began a long war and annihilated the Genoese troops.

Corsica was French for the first time, but not for long. It was divided between partisans of France and of Genoa– among them most of Vanina's family. A few years later, suspecting his wife of treason, Sampiero intercepted the vessel taking her to Genoa. Vanina was brought back to the South of France and was solemnly condemned to death... by her husband. She accepted her sentence, but asked to die by his hands. After kissing her, Sampiero put a scarf around her neck and strangled her!

Those were brutal times, and hearts were merciless. Legend has it that this tragedy –reminiscent of King Henry VIII of England having two of his wives and queens of England, Anne Boleyn and Catherine Howard, beheaded– inspired Shakespeare's play Othello. For a long time, the French and all of Europe only knew of Corsica through the name of Sampiero Corso.

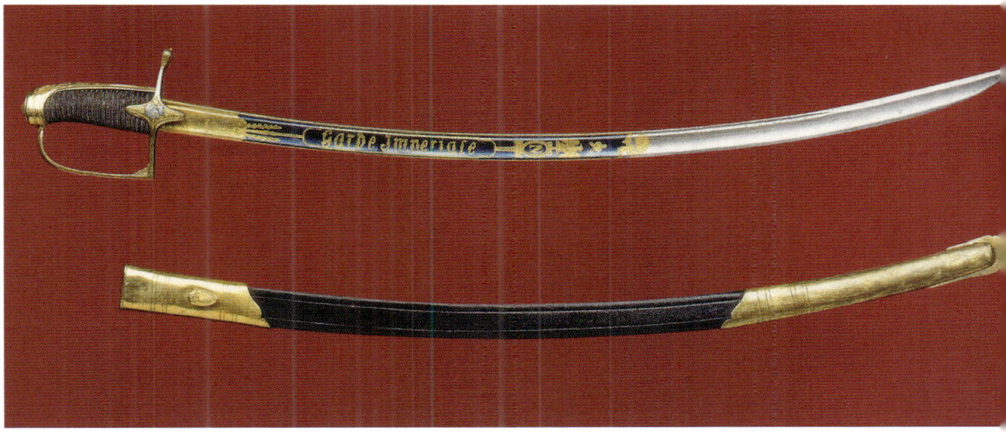

A sword belonging to the Maréchal de France Philippe-Antoine d'Ornano and its scabbard, housed today in the national museum, Les Invalides.

Alphonse d'Ornano, the swordsman of Henri III and Henri IV

Alphonse d'Ornano. King Henri IV made Sampiero Corso's son the first Maréchal de France of the family (anonymous portrait).

Alphonse d'Ornano, Sampiero's son, had inherited his mother's name and the cause and prestige his father had fought so hard for. Taking up where his father left off, he tried for two years to maintain the fight against the Genoese. However, Corsicans were worn out and exhausted after these endless battles, and eventually with the advice of France he signed a treaty with the Republic of Genoa. He left his native island, never to return, and set off with 200 men for a new life in France where he was brought up as a "child of honour of the princes of France" and became the Dauphin's page. Following in his father's footsteps, Alphonse, who made his comeback during the Wars of Religion, remained Catholic and sided with the royal banner. Welcomed with open arms by Charles IX (4) and Catherine de Medici (5), he offered them his talent as a warlord, his formidable "Corsican Company", strengthened by the successive raising of men from his native island, and his loyalty. Weakened, deceived, disobeyed whichever way they turned, the royal party wavered, but it could count on the

4. The reign of the second son of Henri II was marked by the massacre of the Protestants during Saint-Barthélemy's day, August 24th 1572.

5. Born in Florence in 1519, the widow of Henri II governed France during the reign of her sons François II, Charles IX and partly that of Henri III, in the middle of the religious wars that ripped apart the country. The "black widow" as she is referred to, remains a controversial historical figure in the history of France despite her policy of conciliation between the enemy camps destroying the country.

continual support of the Corsican leader and his men. For almost half a century, Alphonse would be the monarchy's most loyal supporter in the South of France. Ornano and his band were relentlessly laying siege on a city here, undertaking garrison duty there, providing assistance elsewhere, or covering a retreat.

Never ending, exhausting and repetitive work... Alphonse was wounded twice, in 1573 and 1575, in front of the city of Sommières, a Protestant stronghold in Provence. A thousand Catholics were killed during the siege. Alphonse was among the wounded; his right leg was seriously injured during an assault. Three years later, he was struck by a shot from a harquebus. He remained standing until the end of combat, and visited a few of the wounded before collapsing on a stretcher.

"Alphonse showed his dedication to public affairs during one of the many plagues that decimated Bordeaux in 1604. Refusing to leave the city, he helped his people."

Ornano remained inextricably tied to the party of Henri III [6] and then Henri IV [7], once Protestant, whom he assisted in recapturing his kingdom from the Catholic Leaguers, his fellow-believers. The new king, who gave Ornano and his men the French nationality, paid him this ultimate compliment:
"I'm better served by you, who were not born as my subject, than I am by those to whom I do the most good!"

On February 7th 1594, he recaptured Lyon by surprise, the kingdom's second largest city that had fallen into the hands of the Duke of Savoie, a feat which earned him the promotion to the rank of Knight of the Holy Spirit, an order reserved for the highest French nobility. On September 5th, Alphonse d'Ornano received the Maréchal de France's baton from the King.

---

6. The last King (1574-1589) from the House of Valois died, stabbed, by the monk Jacques Clément. He bequeathed his kingdom to the Protestant prince, Henri de Navarre, who later became Henri IV.

7. The first from the House of Bourbons to ascend to the throne, he converted to Catholicism to reconquer his kingdom, which he would pacify thanks to the edict of Nantes (1598) signed between the Catholics and Protestants. He was preparing a war against Spain when he was assassinated in 1610.

Peace had been restored and in 1599 King Henri IV bestowed on Alphonse the title of Lieutenant-General of Guyenne, a position reserved solely for members of the Royal family. Elected mayor of Bordeaux two years later, he proved to be a good administrator. He showed his dedication to public affairs in 1604 during one of the many plagues that decimated the city by refusing to leave Bordeaux, as was customary in high society. He continued to oversee the works in the city ensuring fresh water supplies for the sick inhabitants. Having cheated the Plague, Alphonse d'Ornano would finally succumb to the rare 'Stone Man' syndrome, dying in Paris on January 21st 1610. He was sorely missed by King Henri IV, who was stabbed to death by the catholic fanatic Ravaillac a few months later on May 14th, as well as by the inhabitants of Bordeaux. In this major seaport, a street and a gate perpetuate his memory. A street also bears his name in Lyon, the second of the two great cities whose destiny he marked.

The port of Bordeaux in the 16th century. Alphonse d'Ornano was Mayor of the town at the beginning of the 17th century, notably during the period of the plague of 1604.

The tragic fate of Jean-Baptiste d'Ornano

Jean-Baptiste d'Ornano. Made Maréchal de France by King Louis XIII, he was imprisoned at the Château of Vincennes where he died in a mysterious manner (anonymous portrait).

Tall, good-looking and witty, Jean-Baptiste d'Ornano, like his father and grandfather before him, was a talented soldier with a love of glory, and power, to which he was getting forever closer. Taking up the reins of his father, he headed the regiment of the Corse Guards at the age of sixteen! He was later a reluctant participant in the plot in which Concini, the Maréchal d'Ancre and a favourite of the then Regent, Marie de Medici, was assassinated following the desire of King Louis XIII [(8)], who also at the age of sixteen, wanted to seize power from his mother. When Concini was killed in April 1617, Jean-Baptiste d'Ornano was the first to announce to the young king that his orders had been carried out: "My Lord, it is done," he told him curtly, before opening a window of the Louvre, raising the young king in his arms and offering him to the cheers of the crowd so as to reassure it. His participation, would make him a mortal enemy of Marie de Medici and of Cardinal de Richelieu, leading to tragic consequences for him in the future.

Meanwhile, the ascent of Jean-Baptiste continued. He became head of the House of Gaston, the younger brother of Louis XIII. 'Monsieur', as the king's younger brother was always called, was

8. Louis XIII, King of France from 1610 to 1643. With Cardinal de Richelieu, he reduced the power of the aristocracy as well as that of the Protestants, and weakened the influence of the House of Habsburg (who up until then were dominating Europe).

the heir to the throne because the marriage between Louis XIII and Anne of Austria [9] had yet to produce an heir and the future Louis XIV [10] would be born much later. Jean-Baptiste was henceforth head of a royal household of two hundred men and at the beginning of 1626, thanks to the influence of Monsieur, he became Maréchal. This promotion unsettled the King, alarmed at the consequences of such a rise to power. The Cardinal de Richelieu retorted:

"It is no more difficult to imprison a Maréchal de France than any other gentleman"

Jean-Baptiste d'Ornano was a man of war but also of culture and spared no pains in educating his protégé, and surrounding him with the prominent writers, artists and scientists of the day. However, dangerous political games were afoot, revolving around the King's brother. Jean-Baptiste became involved in a conspiracy to remove not only Cardinal de Richelieu but also Louis XIII himself, who was of weak health, and marry off his wife Anne of Austria to Monsieur.

The government of France was at stake and the aristocracy was seeking revenge against the rise of royal power. In his *Memoires*, the powerful Cardinal de Richelieu [11] wrote, maybe exaggerating:

"The Maréchal d'Ornano was plotting something big."

The plot was immediately thwarted by Louis XIII and the Cardinal de Richelieu. Jean-Baptiste d'Ornano was imprisoned in the

9. Sister to King Philippe IV of Spain. Louis XIII was wary of her throughout his reign. The birth of an heir, the future Louis XIV, made her regent of the Kingdom upon the death of her husband. She governed France along with Cardinal Mazarin in the troubled times of the Fronde until her son came of age.

10. Louis XIV, born in 1638, King of France from 1643 to 1715. The 72 year reign of the "Sun King", builder of the château of Versailles, was one of the longest and most brilliant in the history of France.

11. This fearful character, the Cardinal Duke of Richelieu (1585-1642), was known as the 'First Minister' to Louis XIII, he reinforced royal power, preparing the advent of absolute monarchy. He was later immortalised in Alexandre Dumas', *Three Musketeers*, in 1844.

Vincennes dungeons and died mysteriously on September 2nd 1626 at the age of forty-six, while his trial was being prepared. Did he die of natural causes in his prison, famous for its bad conditions? Was he eliminated, poisoned, strangled or beheaded? When the family retrieved the body, they found that his head had been reattached to the body with gold thread. In any case, his death ruled out the prospect of a trial that would have been embarrassing to the Queen and the King's brother.

The King had the body of Jean-Baptiste d'Ornano returned to his widow, Countess of Montlaur, who buried him in a mausoleum, which can still be seen in a chapel in Aubenas, Ardèche [12] of which he was Baron.

The end of one who had been the private tutor of the King's brother and Maréchal de France, so close to the supreme power, remains a mystery. In my eyes, the answer lies in the first four verses of a poem attached to his funeral pall:

> "I would have been very happy, if imitating my father,
> If I had served only our King.
> For from the moment I belonged to his brother,
> Trouble and misfortune overcame me."

The secret behind the strength of his grandfather Sampiero, his father Alphonse and their distant relative, Philippe-Antoine, lay in being the faithful arm of their sovereign.

12. Ancient province of the Vivarais, this picturesque county in the South-East of France is situated on the right banks of the Rhône.

Clockwise from top left: François Ier, Henri IV, Ann of Austria and Louis XIII, three kings and a queen of France who played an important role in the d'Ornano history.

Maréchal de France, keeper of the King's horses

The Maréchal was in charge of the royal stables at the court of the Merovingian kings. During the Middle Ages, he was the man who walked the horses, commanded the vanguard of the royal army and struck the first blows to the enemy –and was above all a man of the king, a man of his "house", almost family. At the beginning of the Bourbon dynasty, during the reign of Louis XIII, the Cardinal de Richelieu made the Maréchal de France the highest military rank. It came immediately below royal princes, with the title of Grand Officer of the Crown.

The "baton" (stick) became the quintessential and very prestigious insignia of the rank of Maréchal de France particularly under Louis XIII. It is a wooden cylinder twenty inches long (fifty-two centimeters), covered with royal blue silk, and embroidered with fleurs-de-lys (eagles during the Empire, stars today). The proud motto: *"Terror belli, decus paciis"* inscribed round the top of the baton –meaning: It inspires terror in times of war, and respect in times of peace.

The baton of the Maréchal de France Philippe-Antoine d'Ornano, adorned with imperial eagles.

Philippe-Antoine d'Ornano, the glory of two emperors

After the death of Jean-Baptiste, the d'Ornano family disappeared from the history of France through the cruel hands of a queen and a cardinal! However, the family would rise again less than two centuries later with Philippe-Antoine d'Ornano, a distant descendant of the elder branch of Orlando d'Ornano. The fifth son of Ludovico d'Ornano and Isabelle Bonaparte, only daughter of Napoleon Bonaparte, great uncle of Emperor Napoleon, was born on January 17th 1784 in Ajaccio.

This young Corsican had a few strings to his bow: his love of the homeland, rooted in his family and in an island that had become permanently French in 1769, the military tradition and his kinship to Napoleon Bonaparte, of whom he was a direct cousin. Although the monarchy was gone, the Revolution had equalized opportunities and conduct –and the path the future emperor was taking would open up a bright future for the young Corsican. His destiny would be resolutely and exclusively Napoleonic, as the life of Philippe-Antoine d'Ornano would be constantly interlaced with the great Napoleonic adventure.

Philippe-Antoine d'Ornano, one of Napoleon I's youngest generals, named Maréchal de France by Napoleon III, the third in the family (portrait by Jean-Adophe Beaucé).

The military career of my father Guillaume's great-grandfather began quickly and enthusiastically with the Italian campaign, the crossing of the Great St. Bernard Pass, the heady victory at Marengo [13] and the frantic gallop along the Alp valleys in pursuit of the Austrian cavalry. Then there was the expedition to Santo Domingo (now Haiti) [14] led by Leclerc, the brother-in-law of Napoleon, of whom he was Chief of Staff, to quash the revolt of the island's slaves led by the legendary Toussaint Louverture. This expedition, which also involved the Polish regiments, was a fiasco, particularly as the French troops were decimated by yellow fever. One night, d'Ornano and seven young staff officers took the terrible oath to make one another their heirs in the event of misfortune. Three months later, Philippe-Antoine found himself the sad owner of the personal belongings of his seven comrades. Just like his ancestor Alphonse during the Plague in Bordeaux, death was not on the cards for him.

“ *The young Philippe-Antoine had many strings to his bow: his love of the homeland, rooted in his family and in an island that had become permanently French in 1769, the military tradition and his kinship to Napoleon Bonaparte, of whom he was a direct cousin.”*

Upon returning to France, Philippe-Antoine spent seven years as Chief of Staff to General Berthier, the War Minister. He proved to be brilliant and effective, so much so that the Emperor himself presented him with one of his first Legions of Honour and appointed him commander of the Third Battalion of Corsican Rifles. The d'Ornanos were back! For fourteen years, he revived the fate of the famous Sampiero Corso and of Alphonse d'Ornano on the battlefields of France and Europe.

Philippe-Antoine was named Count of the Empire in 1808, taking part in several campaigns against Spain, and became, at the age of twenty-

---

13. Napoleon Bonaparte's victory in Italy against the Austrian Imperial army in 1800.

14. A French colony situated on the Eastern side of the Island of Hispaniola, after the revolt in 1804 by its black population it became independent under the name Haiti.

Named at Austerlitz: “*The batallion of the Corsican Rifles, led by their commander d'Ornano, behaved as bravely as the most experienced army corps.*”

Named at Iena: “*The Corsicans have behaved superbly and have assailed the walls of the city…*”

Named at Lübeck: “*The Corsicans soldiers advanced like lightening…*” “*The highest compliments to their commander d'Ornano.*”

seven, one of the youngest brigadier generals. General and Count at the age of twenty-seven-how far would Philippe-Antoine have gone if the Empire had lasted?
"This is indeed a very young general," said the Empress Marie-Louise when he was introduced to her by her husband! "It is true, but he is already an old soldier, " the Emperor replied.

Once again, during the Russian campaign he avoided near death. While the French army was retreating during the terrible Russian winter, he was hit by a cannonball while riding his horse. Philippe-Antoine was left for dead among the bodies of men and horses in the ice and snow on the viciously cold night. Next morning, his aide de camp came to collect the body –to his amazement the General was still breathing! Napoleon immediately dispatched his personal surgeon. A carriage was needed to carry him, but only the Emperor's "landau" was available.

In charge of the cuirassiers (mounted cavalry), during the retreat from Russia.

"Take it," said Napoleon, "I will go on foot."

The 1812 military campaign in Russia with the taking of Moscow before this terrible retreat in the depths of winter, would ultimately lead, along with the Spanish war, to the fall of the Napoleonic Empire which had dominated Europe for more than a decade. However, after the 1814 campaign and before Napoleon's exile to the island of Elba, the Emperor entrusted Philippe-Antoine with the decisive command of the Imperial Guard which protected the capital.

The period that followed was difficult for Philippe-Antoine. With Napoleon's exile, he had joined the newly-restored king Louis XVIII, from the House of Bourbons. However, Napoleon's return from exile in 1815, resulting in the so called "Hundred days" (15), would again lead Philippe-Antoine to re-join his cousin Napoleon's side.

Philippe-Antoine, who Napoleon had intended to make Maréchal de France, did not take

15. This period from March to June, 1815 designated the return to power of Napoleon from exile on the Island of Elba and which came to an end with the Battle of Waterloo. The Emperor abdicated definitively and was imprisoned by the English on the island of Saint Helena, in the South Atlantic, where he died in 1821.

Napoleon's farewell at Fontainebleau, the April 20th 1814, with 5th from the right of the Emperor, Philippe-Antoine d'Ornano.

part in the ultimate battle at Waterloo. He was wounded by a bullet in the chest in a duel with General Bonnet who had challenged his military ability. The papers had said that he was dead - again. Who knows what might have happened had he led the cavalry?

However, rejoining Napoleon put him on the Bourbons' blacklist when they returned to power after Napoleon's ultimate defeat at Waterloo. He was taken prisoner and exiled to Belgium, before rallying to the new regime. "A soldier," d'Ornano said "serves his country and not a government."

Now a public figure, he resumed his career as Commander of the military regions in 1828. He was made a peer of France under the July Monarchy [16], and became an MP for Indre-et-Loire under the Second Republic. He acquired the Château de La Branchoire, in the Loire valley, henceforth rooting our family in the centre of France. But his heart was forever elsewhere, with the urn which held the heart of Marie Walewska, his beloved wife. "As long as he lived," said my father emotionally, "my great-grandfather was never separated from that urn, his most precious possession."

The last years of Philippe-Antoine's life were more than glorious. With the return of the Empire under Napoleon III [17], he was made the executor of Napoleon's will, Grand Chancellor of the Order of the Legion of Honour created by his cousin Napoleon, before being appointed governor of the Invalides. On April 2nd 1861, the remains of Emperor Napoleon I were transferred to the marble tomb erected by Louis Visconti under the dome

16. The reign of Louis-Philippe Ist, King of the French between 1830 and 1848 after the fall of Charles IX during the three days 27th, 28th and 29th of July 1830 which saw the uprising of the people of Paris.
17. Napoleon's nephew and French Emperor from 1852 to 1870, he modernised and developed France, but his defeat by Prussia in 1870 led to the fall of his regime and the accession of the Third Republic.

of the Invalides. After the ceremony, Emperor Napoleon III promoted Philippe-Antoine d'Ornano, last of the generals of the Revolution and of the Empire, to Maréchal de France, the third d'Ornano to hold the title. He died two years later, on October 13th 1863, at the Invalides, where his body rests to this day in the crypt of the Maréchaux de France, very close to the dome which houses the remains of the Emperor.

The d'Ornanos today

"Michel and I donated all the archives, collection of swords, maps, decorations, family portraits – including the painting of Marie Walewska, Countess d'Ornano by Gérard, patiently collected by my father, to the Army Museum of the Invalides."

When my grandfather died, my father was the youngest of three brothers. The eldest Philippe, a writer, author of several books on the family history, including one on Marie Walewska, was then aged 25, the second, Jean-Baptiste, was 22 and like my father would pursue a career in cosmetics. In 1920 my grandmother died prematurely, worn out by grief, at the age of 62.

But it was my father who rebuilt the family through hard work and an attachment to the history of the d'Ornanos. As soon as he was financially able, he would constantly buy back portraits, objects, documents of any kind connected with his ancestors. Michel and I have followed in his footsteps.

After his death in 1985, My brother and I, according to his wish, donated all the archives, collections of swords, maps, decorations, family portraits –including the painting of Marie Walewska, Countess d'Ornano by Gérard [18], patiently collected by my father, to the Museum of the Invalides, where the opening of the d'Ornano Gallery coincided with the publishing of a book *Les maréchaux de la famille d'Ornano* [The Marshals of the d'Ornano Family] –a story intimately connected with the history of France and Corsica– and the final chapters of which are still to be written!

18. François Gérard (1770-1837) a French neoclassical painter raised in Rome, renowned for his portraits including those of Napoleon and other prominent figures of his time.

Seated under the bust and the arms of my ancestor, Philippe-Antoine d Ornano.

Chapter 3

A forest in the heart of France

Guillaume d'Ornano and Armand Petitjean, the two founders of Lancôme, in the 1930s.

“We are in the Indre Valley, in the heart of France. My mother Elisabeth loved this place. She suggested the name Lancosme for the company that her husband Guillaume and his partner Armand Petitjean were creating. Thus began the d'Ornanos journey into the world of cosmetics.”

In the Indre valley right in the heart of France, lies a forest, a vast area of several thousand hectares located in the region of La Brenne known as the "Land of one thousand lakes". This forest, with its Louis XIII castle, is called Lancosme.

My mother Elisabeth loved this place and suggested that the company founded by Armand Petitjean and her husband Guillaume be called Lancosme. Thus began the d'Ornanos' journey into the world of cosmetics.

The legacy of François Coty

My father had already gained some experience in the world of perfume a few years earlier when, upon returning from Poland he met François Coty, one of the greatest French perfumers. Joseph Marie François Spoturno, his real name, was born in Ajaccio in May 1874. He was orphaned at an early age and moved to Paris. In 1900 he married, and took his wife's name Coti, changed to Coty, which seemed easier to pronounce and more elegant than his own.

François Coty, who according to his business card was "an industrialist, an artist, technician, economist, financier, sociologist", invented the modern French perfume industry. He realized that perfume, until then reserved for the elite, could become a popular product, industrially produced due to discoveries in synthetic chemistry. Natural essences can now be combined with synthetic products on an industrial scale.

As well as being a businessman, François Coty was also the nose behind many hugely successful perfumes with evocative names including La Rose Jacqueminot, Origan, Ambre Antique, Muguet, Lilas Blanc, Iris, Chypre (after which have been named the Cyprus family aromas). Some were available in bottles designed by Baccarat.

Coty had flair and a sense of what was to become known as marketing. He proclaimed: "Offer a woman the best product you can make, present it in a beautifully simple yet perfect bottle with impeccable taste, at a reasonable price, and it will start the greatest business the world has ever known".

Francois Coty was the first to sell his products in department stores and distributed them not only in New York, but all over the world. He invented perfume in small sizes, which he sold to the American soldiers who came to save the Allies. In 1922 Coty took to politics with far right opinions and bought a newspaper *Le Figaro* which he located at the Rond-Point des Champs-Élysées. Six years later he created a very popular tabloid, *L'Ami du Peuple*, of which my father became president. François Coty died in 1934 having created the modern French and American perfume industry. The Coty Group still exists on the other side of the Atlantic, a conglomerate which distributes a portfolio of brands including Calvin Klein, Balenciaga, Viviane Westwood, Marc Jacobs, to name just a few.

François Coty, the father of modern French perfumery.

The creation of Lancôme with Armand Petitjean

When François Coty died his business was immediately sold. It was on the Louveciennes station platform, near Paris, coming back from his funeral that Armand Petitjean, his managing director, and my father decided to create a new company with the perfumers' French team. Armand Petitjean was a self-made man and adventurer who had travelled far and wide, particularly to South America. My uncle Jean-Baptiste, a business executive at Coty, would join them too. Having actively contributed to the expansion of Coty and with the experience they had gained, Armand Petitjean and Guillaume d'Ornano took the risk of embarking on this new adventure. Armand was already 50 years old and my father was 41. The company was established on February 19th 1935 with four shareholders, Armand Petitjean, Guillaume d'Ornano, Max Everaert and the Prince de Carini.

It was my mother's idea to name the company after the Lancosme Forest, which was near our home. The company was registered under the name of Lancosme on February 16th, but a lawsuit was filed by a Parisian pharmacist for using his name! In May the "s" was dropped and replaced with a circumflex accent on the "o", hence the now famous name of Lancôme.

The two founders did not wish to make the same mistake as François Coty who, under the influence of his partners, pushed the business toward mass distribution. Lancôme, launched during the economic crisis, started out magnificently. Registered at the last minute for the World Expo held in Brussels from April to November 1935, the company introduced five prestigious perfumes: Conquête, Chypre, Tropiques, Tendres Nuits and Bocages, in Romesnil crystal flacons and in boxes decorated with designs by Draeger. The dazzling showcase of the World Expo and the brand's luxury baroque style, which contrasted with the rather austere 1930s, launched Lancôme on the international stage.

> "*Offer a woman the best product you can make, present it in a beautifully simple yet perfect bottle with impeccable taste, at a reasonable price, and it will be the birth of the greatest business the world has ever known.*"
>
> *François Coty.*

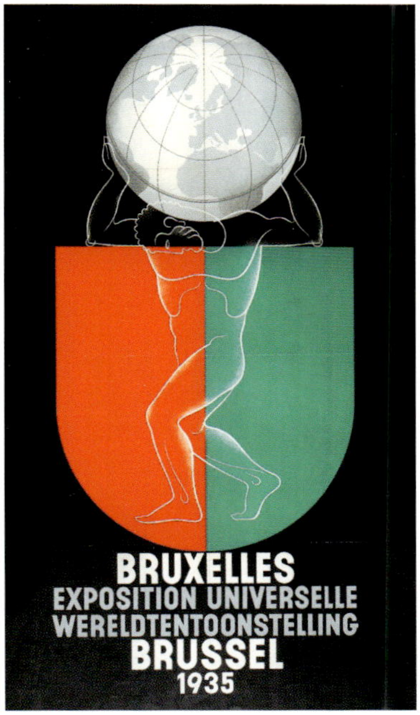

The following year, Armand Petitjean developed a nourishing cream containing horse serum, proteins and vitamins, and gave it the particularly appropriate name of Nutrix. It became a bestseller for years. In 1937, another stroke of genius: the soft French Rose lipstick, which lasted thirty years. Then in 1942 the Lancôme School was established at 9 Boulevard des Italiens in Paris, to train high quality "technicians", instructors and ambassadors who would represent the name and expertise of Lancôme worldwide.

Poster from the International Exhibition in Brussels from April to November 1935, during which five Lancôme perfumes were presented to the public for the first time.

Guillaume d'Ornano's three ambitions

With Armand Petitjean, my father was one of the two pillars of the early success of Lancôme. In 1939 he was joined by his brother Jean-Baptiste, who had not invested any capital, but had helped to set up the business and was working for Coty. Hard-working and intelligent, my father set himself three aims to revive the d'Ornano name: succeed in business, have a political career and run newspapers. The first had been very successfully achieved; the other two would succeed later on with my brother Michel.

Guillaume d'Ornano began his political career in Indre in the 1920s, in the heart of the former Berry; a region dear to the writer George Sand and often quoted in her books. The family rented a property, Jarzay Manor, on the edge of the small village of Moulins-sur-Céphons, and later purchased La Pointerie estate near Châteauroux.

La Pointerie, at the gates of Châteauroux.

For fifteen years, in the post-war period, this quiet, uneventful town located in the centre of France acted as the HQ of a large US base of almost 8,000 men, part of NATO before the withdrawal of General de Gaulle.

As Mayor of Moulins-sur-Céphons from 1925 to 1944, and Councillor for the district of Levroux from 1928 to 1945, my father was, unlike François Coty, a moderate Republican. He stood for parliament twice, in 1928 and again in 1932, for the left wing Republicans, that is the moderate right. However, he was up against a local political figure, the Socialist Max Hymans, who went on to be Minister several times in the 1930s, and, who after the Second World War, became head of the French airline Air France. The 1928 elections proved to be extremely close. The difference became bigger four years later in 1932.

“Hard-working and intelligent, my father set himself three aims to revive the d'Ornano name: succeed in business, have a political career and run newspapers.”

Somewhat discouraged, my father abandoned politics and devoted most of his time to work and his family. His withdrawal from politics would prove to be a fundamental turning point in my family's destiny, a stroke of luck for us –from then on all my father's energy went towards his family and the cosmetic business!

Guillaume d'Ornano fought in World War One as a captain and served for two years in the Second World War. In 1944 he was involved in the liberation of the Berry region when he and my mother convinced the German General Henning Botho Elster and his 20,000 men to surrender. Retreating northward, the general had commandeered our La Pointerie property for his HQ. Under constant attack, both men and weapons were exhausted, while the destruction of the bridges over the Loire River made a retreat northwards very unlikely. General Elster was neither a hardliner, nor bloodthirsty, nor a Nazi. This Rhinelander, as we later learned, was linked to the conspirators who attempted to assassinate Hitler on July 20th 1944; he now ordered his troops to avoid reprisals and violent acts.

Guillaume d'Ornano during World War I.

As my mother was Polish she spoke fluent German and played the role of a perfect and wise interpreter. Her presence was decisive in the discussion which, on September 6th 1944, gradually led General Elster to surrender. It was my mother and father who were the first to show the German warrior that his efforts were in vain and persuaded him to choose the only reasonable solution, surrender. My father pointed out in our courtyard the pitiful condition of his troops:
"General, are you sure to be able to take your men further North? Are you sure they will follow you? They are in no condition to fight and it will end in bloodshed, you must surrender.

In theory, a German general never surrenders. But my mother and father were dealing with a man who had values, was receptive, intelligent, and sensitive to saving lives. Gradually, General Elster came around to my parents arguments, "I cannot surrender without valid reasons and solid guarantees. I must make my men understand this; I want to consult my officers as I need their agreement."

General Elster laid down his conditions:
"I want to surrender to a regular army, with the honours of war; my soldiers will hand over their arms at the last moment to Americans, not Communists or Russians."

Elisabeth and Guillaume d'Ornano.

Further meetings were held, on the 8th and 9th of September, at the Duke of Maillé's castle in Châteauneuf-sur-Cher. When the news reached the Americans, no one could believe it: "20,000 Germans and their general surrendering all at once? Impossible!" However, on the afternoon of September 10th, at the sub-prefecture of Issoudun, General Elster, accompanied by two officers, signed the surrender to the Allied forces before General Robert C. Macon, Commander of the 83rd US Infantry, Colonel Baker, Chief of Staff to General Simpson, Commander of the 9th US army and the English Major McStafford – all three parachuted for the occasion –and the FFI [(1)] Colonel Chomel. The latter accepted that the surrender was to be to US troops. Upon the request of the Resistance, the confirmation of the surrender took place the next day in the town hall of the small village of Arçay.

The surrender of Elster's 20,000 men lined up in front of the American troops, September 16th 1944 at the bridge of Beaugency, in the Loire Valley; my father and my mother played a key role in this episode.

With 19,600 men, two generals, 470 officers, 20 canons, 14 AA canons, 337 guns, 24,000 arms and 600 cars lined up, the fighting ceased. To paraphrase Churchill's famous phrase about the Battle of Britain, 'never have so many men surrendered to so few...' The Germans kept their weapons until the official surrender which took place on 16th September on Beaugency Bridge on the south bank of

1. The French Forces of the Interior, an organization assembling all the resistant military movements inside France from 1944.

the Loire, with military honours for the troops. For one moment, we witnessed the incredible sight of Germans and Americans together, the former with their weapons on their shoulders.

This earned General Elster a death sentence in absentia from the War Council of the Reich for "misplaced and dangerous humanity" and the anger of the local FFI's resistance who believed that we were "stealing their Germans from them!" Disarmed by the Americans, imprisoned with his soldiers in Missouri, where some of them considered him a traitor, General Elster was freed in 1947.

The Liberation of France created an exacerbated climate in which the French resistance movement and the proclamation of a country, which pretended to have freed itself from its occupants without the help of the Allies, converged; the episode of General Elster surrendering directly to Americans was hard to swallow.

My father himself was at first accused of stealing a German surrender from the French resistance. After a first trial, he was acquitted by the military court of the 1st Military Region of Paris. He received the 1939-1945 War Cross and was awarded the Legion of Honour with military title for his action on that day. Although the plaque to commemorate the event in Arçay in 1946 wrongly mentions an exclusively Franco-German episode, it was the only example of surrender of an entire German division to US troops. The Surrender of General Elster at Beaugency had also been filmed and tapes of the ceremony were broadcasted in the United States.

By that time, my father and his partner had grown apart. Armand Petitjean, an original and exceptional character, was a despotic, very self-centred man, jealous of his authority. He intended to maintain

Lancôme as a luxury brand, banned any form of advertising, and only desired the perfume branch to be developed abroad, particularly in the United States. My father, younger, with a more modern outlook, did not share such a restrictive approach. That is why, soon after the end of the war, my father Guillaume began to distance himself from his partner and helped my brother and me develop a new business.

My father maintained his share of Lancôme for a few more years and Jean-Baptiste d'Ornano remained with the company, where he was joined by his sons, Rodolphe and Christian. They continued to work for many years for a company that would be eventually sold to the L'Oreal Group, which was at the time seeking to enter the world of luxury cosmetics. Armand-Marcel Petitjean, Armand's son, even though he became president of the company in the early 1960s, was not interested in business. Author of several essays and books from the inter-war period, he became one of the forerunners of ecology in the 1970s. It was again Armand Petitjean who in 1964 with the President of L'Oreal, François Dalle, negotiated the sale of the company he had founded nearly thirty years earlier with my father. I had a lot of respect for François Dalle. This exceptional business man, whom we liked very much, transformed Lancôme into L'Oreal's flagship, a global brand.

"Guillaume d'Ornano received the 1939-1945 War Cross and was awarded the Legion of Honour with military title for his action on September 6th 1944; it was the only example of surrender of an entire German division to US troops."

A page had been turned and a new adventure in cosmetics would start, this time for Michel and for me.

My parents on board the liner Île-de-France *during a transatlantic crossing, in the 1930s.*

Chapter 4

The family bond

Taking my first steps in working life;
to the left: with Michel and my mother Elisabeth.

“My return from Poland, or rather my arrival in France, was not easy. Nothing comes easily, luck and happiness have to be worked on to make them happen.”

My return from Poland, or rather my arrival in France, was not easy. My French was hesitant –I came from elsewhere. But the years spent in Poland with my grandmother in the country had made me physically robust which would prove useful during my remaining childhood and my adolescence.

Michel, my brother, grew up as an only child. He was ten years old when, upon my arrival, I asked him if I could try his bicycle. He said he still needed it and began riding around the house, until out of pure exhaustion he fell off and broke his arm!

Michel and his famous bicycle, at the origin of a memorable episode between the two d'Ornano brothers!

"Luck takes work"

This episode did not prevent us from becoming very close during our adolescence. We loved our parents and their example influenced us both. My father was a poised, precise man, far from mundane. Intelligent, determined, ambitious in a positive way, he was also profoundly humane, with his family as well as his employees. We all respected him. My mother was charismatic, charming and brave. She was a hard working person and as she often said: nothing comes easily, luck and happiness have to be worked at to make them happen.

So we were hard workers and luck would follow! I have had many good times in my life and some not so good, but nothing came easily.

> *"Family is everything to me. I was born under a lucky star, into a family that cherishes tradition."*

As brothers, although we shared the same values, when it came to our personalities we were very different. Methodical, thoughtful, a homebody, Michel also loved race cars. Impetuous, dynamic and socially at ease, I was in my own world. While my brother had little time for socializing, I on the other hand enjoyed meeting people from different walks of life; sports, business, politics or purely varying social circles –it could be in my opinion useful for business or simply enjoyable and interesting. I belonged to several clubs and was on the Jockey Club board. Yet I didn't take my social life too seriously, I was never caught up in the social frenzy, deep down I was a lone wolf who followed my instinct, and have always wanted to be independent. Family has been the most important thing in the world to me and I was extremely happy when I started my own family with Isabelle. Then came my business, my country, nature, shooting and hunting and of course my horses.

Throughout generations, we have been first and foremost a family. Family is everything to me. I was born under a lucky star, into one that cherishes tradition. This legacy entails duties, giving us both a desire to do something meaningful. Our ancestors went to war, we created and developed businesses and were interested in public life, my brother more so than my father and me.

It is in France that I truly learnt French. I attended Saint-Martin school in Pontoise, on the Saint Martin estate. The classrooms and dormitories were situated on this vast property with an ancient Benedictine abbey and a 17th century castle, surrounded by gardens designed by Le Nôtre. We were taught certain principles there, which I hope became inherent in me: trust in men, an open mind, the respect for freedom and the desire to be creative. From there I went on to law school in Paris.

Jean d'Albret perfumes…

I was 20 and Michel was 22. His upbringing had been different to mine: a Berry childhood, the lycée Carnot in Paris, with a philosophy class taught by the famous professor Maurice Merleau-Ponty. For us both our studies were short lived: "You have to work", my father decided. After the war years, our country was still living off ration tickets, was poor and needed rebuilding. In my father's opinion everyone had to "roll up their sleeves" as the famous saying goes.

"One need not hope in order to undertake, nor succeed in order to persevere."

William of Orange.

He lent us the money and in July 1946 Michel and I created a small perfume business, Jean d'Albret. The company had five partners, the three d'Ornanos, Henri Viguier and Hervé de Villette. Such an initiative seems surprising today, but it was very representative of our mentality back then. There was no need to study to set up a business and for us, for me in particular, there was no distance between an idea and its immediate implementation in order to successfully carry out a project. I adopted the famous motto of William of Orange, Stadtholder of Holland that my father (with whom he shared the same initials and the same first name!) passed on to me: "One need not hope in order to undertake, nor succeed in order to persevere".

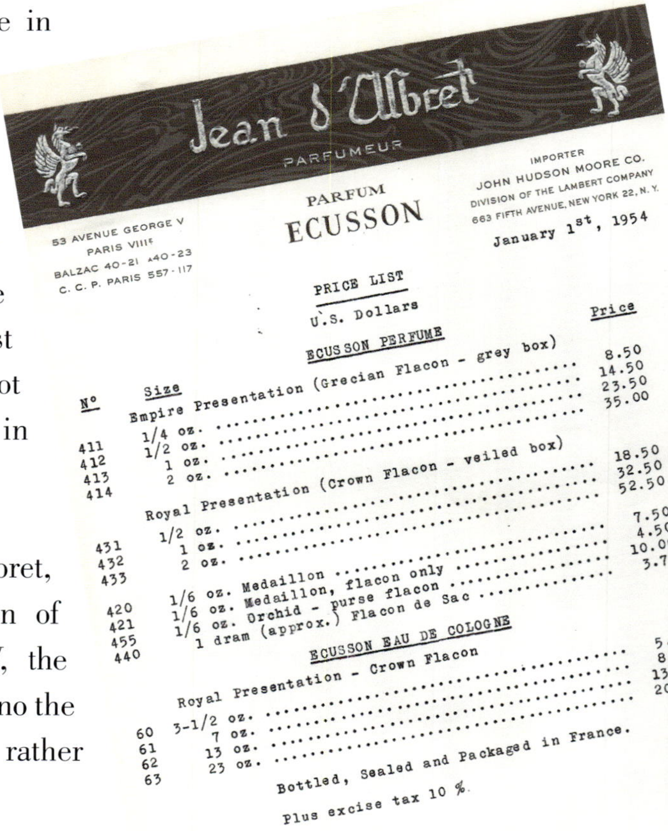

Jean d'Albret

PARFUMEUR

53 AVENUE GEORGE V
PARIS VIIIE
BALZAC 40-21 40-23
C. C. P. PARIS 557-117

PARFUM
ECUSSON

IMPORTER
JOHN HUDSON MOORE CO.
DIVISION OF THE LAMBERT COMPANY
663 FIFTH AVENUE, NEW YORK 22, N. Y.

January 1st, 1954

PRICE LIST

U.S. Dollars

ECUSSON PERFUME

Nº	Size	Price
	Empire Presentation (Grecian Flacon - grey box)	
411	1/4 oz.	8.50
412	1/2 oz.	14.50
413	1 oz.	23.50
414	2 oz.	35.00
	Royal Presentation (Crown Flacon - veiled box)	
431	1/2 oz.	18.50
432	1 oz.	32.50
433	2 oz.	52.50
420	1/6 oz. Medaillon	7.50
421	1/6 oz. Medaillon, flacon only	4.50
455	1/6 oz. Orchid - purse flacon	10.00
440	1 dram (approx.) Flacon de Sac	3.75

ECUSSON EAU DE COLOGNE

Nº	Size	Price
	Royal Presentation - Crown Flacon	
60	3-1/2 oz.	5.00
61	7 oz.	8.50
62	13 oz.	13.50
63	23 oz.	20.00

Bottled, Sealed and Packaged in France.

Plus excise tax 10 %.

My father suggested the name Jean d'Albret, in reference to Jeanne d'Albret, Queen of Navarre and mother of King Henri IV, the sovereign who had made Alphonse d'Ornano the family's first Maréchal de France. A rather

Headings and visuals of the Jean d'Albret perfumes and Orlane products at the beginning of the 1950s.

old-fashioned name, even in France, and to be honest, one that is impossible to pronounce by foreigners! The increasing distance between my father and his partner Petitjean and the early success of Jean d'Albret perfumes with the perfume 'Ecusson' led him, a few years later, to sell his shares in Lancôme and join us. Guillaume d'Ornano of course then ran the business, to which his talent, experience and expertise gave new impetus. He was already over fifty and a wonderful example for our whole family –the father participating in his sons' adventure!

He was assisted by a secretary –as the offices were not heated she came to work in trousers, somewhat revolutionary at the time!– and two young salesmen, my brother and me. From our first offices rue Boissy d'Anglas, we squeezed into a small cramped office on the 7th floor of a building overlooking 12 rue du Faubourg Saint-Honoré, which gave us a well-known, prestigious address. In 1952, we moved to 53 Avenue George V, where we remained for many years. Everything was still to be done, but it was our own company!

At age twenty, I should have done my military service, but I was allowed to postpone it as I was starting a business. However, I finally went, age 25, to Rambouillet, and from there to the well-known officers' school in Saumur. In Rambouillet on weekends, my men were called to serve as beaters at the presidential shoots, which they did not like at all. They used to say:
"It is more dangerous than being sent to Indochina, Sir!"

Like a true d'Ornano, I loved the army, where of course I got on like a house on fire with my fellow Corsicans. They welcomed me warmly from day one. Once I had completed my military service, I returned to our business.

Ecusson, the first Jean d'Albret perfume, was launched in 1946, and it was the first in a long line of names that would continue to grow until the beginning of the 1970s: Rafale, Lavande, Casaque, Classic, Messire, Princesse d'Albret, Eau de Lavande, Odyssée... In those days, unlike today, perfumes were made to last. This was the case for Ecusson, which was sold to the American troops in France as a gift to take home and became an instant success from the start; its fragrance appealed. Available in two forms: scented eau de cologne and eau de toilette, Ecusson also capitalized on the pastel drawings by Pierre Simon, one of the great designers of the time.

Among Jean d'Albret perfumes, Casaque was a reminder of the family's passion for horses and racing. It was created in 1956 especially for the North American market and distributed by Warner-Lambert, with whom we became good friends. They later distributed the Orlane cosmetics. We also had 'Messire' a perfumed range for men, and Lavande and Eau de Lavande fresh and simple, which appealed to many in the rise of modern consumption.

...and Orlane beauty products

With the financial success of Ecusson we were able to launch a range of skincare products at the beginning of the 1950s. Our cosmetic line was given a different name to that of the perfumes. We called it Orlane. Again, there were many legends as to the origin of the name. Some thought it was inspired from the first name of the Duchesse de

Guermantes, Oriane in *A la recherche du temps perdu* [In Search of Lost Time] by Marcel Proust. But like Lancôme, it was again my mother's idea. She simply changed two letters: the "n" in Ornano was replaced with "l" and the final "o" with an "e".

Sitting under the painting of my father by Ricardo Macarron, and in front of Jean d'Albret-Orlane products.

Unlike Jean d'Albret, deeply rooted in a more traditional image, Orlane would be a decidedly scientific and modern brand of luxury cosmetics. Orlane products were formulated in a research laboratory, managed by Egmont Desperrois, a well-known chemical engineer, one of the great names in the post-war French cosmetic world. The Orlane laboratory was a pioneer in the use of new technology to isolate natural ingredients.

In 1953, our research created Crème à la Gelée Royale, the first royal jelly-based cream –with anti-aging properties. Driven by the steady rise in the standard of living, the ever growing desire to stay young and attractive, Crème à la Gelée Royale became an instant and lasting success, followed by the Astral night cream. At that point no one wanted to age anymore! We innovated with advertising campaigns that were very audacious at the time, even avant-garde. To the perfumes and skincare products, we added a line of makeup, also driven by somewhat aggressive advertising. One campaign announced what colour women's lipstick should be that year: "This year, Orlane decrees: your makeup will be beige!"

We went international very early on; the broadest possible worldwide distribution was the only way to establish the quality and reputation of demanding products like ours; this is still true for current and future companies. From 1953 on, not only were we present in Benelux, Italy, the UK and Sweden, but also in the US, following in the footsteps of Jean d'Albret perfumes. My mother and father were in charge of the French market, while Michel and I ran exports. We divided the world between us; my brother managed North Africa, a major client then, North and South America, whilst I was in charge of Western Europe and Japan, the most profitable and dynamic markets at that time.

With my brother Michel, a passion for dogs.

The Common Market had not yet taken off and the success of Orlane in Italy led us to set up a factory in Genoa, on the sea, which supplied some of the European markets. I spent time in Italy and learnt fluent Italian. The ability to see way beyond the borders of our own country, at a time when the world was full of customs' barriers, led us to be appointed French Foreign Trade Advisers and my brother was also on the Board of the National Committee of Foreign Trade.

"Most of our friends were having fun in the nightclubs of Saint Germain-des-Prés, whilst Michel and I were on the road trying to convince the perfumers of the quality of our products."

In 1963 we opened our first skincare center and three years later the Orlane Institute which was both a beauty and training center. In 1968 we launched the B21 Cream which was an immediate success –a very sophisticated formula for the time, combining amino acids and 21 active ingredients!

All the experts said that we were truly revolutionary. Available in a full range of products, B21 cream made Orlane one of the world's top anti-aging specialists. At that time we moved from the factory in Clichy, near Paris, which had become too small, to a very modern facility near Orleans, which would also house our research laboratories.

It was not, of course, an easy start. In those days after the war, roads were bad, there were no highways and the perfumeries had to be visited all over France. But we were young. Most of our friends were having fun in the nightclubs of Saint Germain-des-Prés, whilst Michel and I were on the road trying to convince the perfumers of the quality of our products! As a childhood friend, Bernard Francois Poncet, put it:
"While we danced, Michel and Hubert worked –when we met them at parties they would disappear before midnight, as the next day they would be up at dawn, travelling across the country methodically boasting the quality of their products!"

We drove a Simca 5 along the charming, in those days tree-lined roads, in the beautiful French countryside. Short of money we sometimes accepted an invitation from the perfumers for the night and close friendships were thus established. I often travelled in the North of France, devastated by the war –few hotels, no accommodation. I remember returning during the day to my hotel room and finding it occupied! The landlady's reply to my protests being, "Young man, we rented you the room for the night, not for the day! "

I was a good salesman and had an instinct for business and networking. The clients we visited would not get rid of us easily! My mother used to do these trips for Lancôme during the war when my father was in the army. We inherited her tireless energy and her Polish business sense. Many years later we once again visited some of these perfumers with my wife, when we launched Sisley, and they still remembered my mother's irresistible charm and simplicity. She was generous and always had a present or a kind word for everyone. I can still find, among my papers, very long pages of her handwritten recommendations, which she sent to me when I was young, before I went on these trips.

My mother was a heavy smoker. Unfortunately she died of cancer at age 54 on June 15th 1954. We were devastated but her death strengthened our family ties even more. This great loss, strangely enough would also change the course of our family's destiny, particularly so for my brother Michel, leading him to Normandy.

> *There were many legends as to the origin of the name… like Lancôme, it was again my mother's idea. She simply changed two letters: the 'n' in Ornano was replaced with 'l' and the final 'o' with an 'e'."*

New roots in Normandy

We were worried for my father, now a widower, and we tried to make some changes in his life so as to amuse him. Horse breeding and racing were in the family tradition, so in the summer of 1954 we rented a villa in Deauville, Mirasol. We bought it two years later. My father had already registered his racing colors –red with yellow stripes, yellow sleeves and a red cap –in 1934 in Châteauroux where he was the president of the Racing Society. But it was up north, in Normandy, that his colours would meet with real success, thanks to thoroughbreds, from his own breed or bought in the famous Deauville Horse Sales. In 1957, Guillaume d'Ornano bought Le Haras de Manneville, a stud farm, created by Henri Coulon in 1927. We owned Manneville and its chateau from 1969 to 1982.

Guillaume d'Ornano at the Deauville's races.

During the Orlane era.

At his stud farm in Manneville, Guillaume d'Ornano had several very good horses with which he won many races. Alongside Misti, an exceptional horse, others would represent the red and yellow colours of Guillaume d'Ornano: Crossen, Le Vieux Castel, Moderne, Firstborn, Futuril, Messire –an allusion to the perfume of the same name –and Cabhurst... They all won several races. My father's horses were originally trained by Sylvain Laforge, later by Georges Bridgland, and the steeplechase horses were trained by Joseph Audon. Before dedicating himself to public life, Michel also owned a few good racing horses, one of which was Picfort. Bistouri, one of my sister-in-law Anne's thoroughbreds, won some races as well.

Misti, the star of Guillaume d'Ornano's stud farm

One of the best mares from the stud farm at Manneville was Mist, mother of several winners, in particular Misti, sired by the stallion Méridien. Misti won eight great races and was placed fifteen times. Thanks to Misti, Guillaume d'Ornano's colours triumphed on many racing tracks. At the age of two he won the Prix des Chênes, at three, the Prix Henry Delamarre, at four, the Prix Ganay and the Milan Jockey Club Grand Prix, at five, the Prix Henri Foy, the Prix Cadran and the Ascot Gold Cup in England.

Misti also raced twice across the Atlantic, in Washington, in 1965, but without winning. At Manneville, he proved to be a great stallion, siring Roselière, who won the Prix de Diane, Mistigri, Toulon, and Ambrellita, as well as steeplechase horses, such as Les Roseaux and Roselier, who both won La Grande Course de Haies d'Auteuil (the French classic steeplechase race).

Member of the Jockey Club and the Société d'Encouragement, Guillaume d'Ornano was president of the Pays d'Auge Racing Society from 1971 to 1978, which organized Le Prix de Clairfontaine-Deauville. He thus became a well-known figure in the racing world and one of the leading personalities of Deauville, where he was well known for his gracious manners and his hospitality at Villa Mirasol. After his death in 1985, Le Prix de la Cote Normande was renamed in his memory 'Prix Guillaume d'Ornano'. Restricted to three-year-old horses and run on the La Touques racetrack, the prize now amounts to €400,000.

At the races with Michel and Egmont Desperrois, Head of Research for Orlane, then Sisley, he was also passionate about horses.

Michel, my brother

Half-Parisian, half-Berichon, the d'Ornanos made a name for themselves along the Normandy coast, in Deauville. But that was only the beginning. My brother, Michel, used to say that he was born on the day my father was elected mayor of Moulins-sur-Céphons! During the political campaigns with Guillaume d'Ornano, he discovered he had a passion for politics. After the sudden death of Robert Fossorier, the then Mayor of Deauville, we were asked if one of us would like to run for Mayor there. Michel was interested –"They wanted a Parisian mayor, just like my predecessor," my brother said.

His was a successful political career, together with Anne, his wife, daughter of the Marquis de Contade, whom he married in 1960 in their beautiful Château de Montgefrois. A few years later he was elected Member of Parliament and became one of the two lieutenants

of Valery Giscard d'Estaing, alongside another political figure of Polish origin, Michel Poniatowski. My brother was involved in the foundation of the Republican Independents Party. He was elected MP for the Calvados in 1967 and continued to be re-elected up until his death. As with his first election in Deauville, the death of the former Member of Parliament opened up the way for him. Michel helped the Independent Republican movement and its young leader, Valery Giscard d'Estaing, become an alternative to the traditional right wing party. He successfully managed his presidential campaign following the unexpected death of President Pompidou. Valéry Giscard d'Estaing was elected President of France in May 1974.

With Valéry Giscard d'Estaing, President of the Republic from 1974 to 1981, and my brother Michel, one of his closest political lieutenants, Minister three times.

After being one of the very influential men in politics, under the VGE presidency, Michel went on to occupy prominent portfolios –he held successive positions as Minister of Industry and Research, Culture and Environment and lastly Environment and Quality of Life.

Michel's only failure was the election for the City of Paris. During a shooting weekend in Rambouillet in 1976, the President took me aside on the Saturday evening and told me he planned to ask Michel to run for Mayor of Paris. It would be the first election by popular vote in the capital for almost two centuries. Since the French Revolution the City of Paris had the dubious privilege of being run by an unelected official, the Préfet de la Seine –as Adolphe Thiers had said, "We cannot leave such a large city to the fate of an election!". He asked me to try to convince my brother to accept.

On our way back from Rambouillet the following evening, Isabelle and I attended a dinner ending the yearly Perfumers Conference in a restaurant in the Bois de Boulogne. Being Minister of Industry at the time, Michel was there to deliver the closing speech. Before dinner I told my brother of the President's wish. His immediate reply was:

"I cannot refuse, but I will not win because Paris is held by the Gaullist Party".

The campaign started off normally for Michel in November 1976 – he ran under the banner "Protection de Paris" which united the Republican Independents and the Center parties. Jacques Chirac was then Prime Minister and had founded the neo-Gaullist party RPR. In January Chirac decided to resign and in turn run for the position of Mayor of Paris. His relationship with VGE had become very difficult. With strong support from the Gaullist party and the media, Jacques Chirac won the election on March 20th 1977 and thus became the first elected Mayor of Paris since 1789. Michel having decided not to run in Deauville, Anne his wife, ran and was easily elected. From then on, for more than twenty years, she was brilliantly re-elected, each time, in the first round.

During the 1980s, which saw the rise to power, first of the socialist President François Mitterrand, then of a coalition government led by Jacques Chirac, Michel returned to his political roots. In 1979 he was elected President of the General Council of Calvados, and from 1983 to 1986 head of the Basse Normandie region. He was also president of the Finance Commission in Parliament.

However, under Mitterrand's socialist presidency Michel was getting bored. In the 1990s he turned his attention to the press, our father's other passion! With the press tycoon Robert Hersant, he set up a profitable media business in the newly free Central European countries (after the fall of the Berlin Wall), particularly in Poland, where he bought on behalf of the Hersant Group the important daily *Rzeczposplita*.

"Michel and Anne d'Ornano significantly modernised Deauville, whilst maintaining its cachet. Thanks to them it became fashionable again."

Tragically, Michel died in a traffic accident in Saint Cloud on March 8th 1991, at the age of 67. My brother still had so much more to achieve! He left behind his wife, Anne, and their two children, a daughter Catherine and Jean-Guillaume their son who has now taken over a newspaper company, the Option Finance Group, publisher of financial publications.

Anne remained mayor of Deauville for 24 years and President of the General Council of Calvados until 2011. The so-called "Duke of Normandy" and his wife left a lasting mark on Deauville, on the department and the region, a bit like Alphonse d'Ornano in Bordeaux. It is thanks to my brother that the motorway link to Deauville from Paris was built. The new football stadium in the city of Caen bears his name.

Michel and Anne significantly modernized Deauville, whilst maintaining its cachet. Known as a seaside resort, racing and weekend destination, it had been somewhat dormant since the Roaring Twenties. Thanks to

Michel and Anne it became fashionable again, even outside the racing season. Deauville is now a town of conferences and festivals, like the very popular American Film Festival of Deauville. From 1977 to 2001, Anne d'Ornano took up the torch and continued his work.

Anne and Michel d'Ornano, a couple in life and in politics. They left their mark in the city of Deauville, the department of Calvados and the Basse Normandie region.

Alone at the helm

My father's increasing age and my brother's political career changed the course and status of Orlane. When he decided he was going to stand for Parliament in 1967 Michel told me:

"It has become impossible for me to continue mixing politics with business. I'm going to dedicate myself exclusively to public life."

Orlane was already a very successful company, employing more than 700 people in France and developing world-renowned products. We had left the cramped quarters in Rue du Faubourg Saint-Honoré long before, for the location at the corner of the Champs-Elysées and Avenue George V where we gradually took over the whole building. Later we would move nearby to a still larger complex on Avenue Marceau. Orlane had become one of the flagships of French luxury cosmetics, in competition with large US companies such as Elizabeth Arden, Estée Lauder or Helena Rubinstein. The US at that time was the world's most important market for beauty products and it was essential to be strongly present there in order to continue growing. As Armand Petitjean summed up in 1946, "There's no future without the United States".

But it is very difficult to penetrate the US market without losing money. American intermediaries are essential in terms of local distribution and it is imperative for a high end cosmetic firm to maintain the right balance between the two risks: too wide a distribution, or too much exclusivity resulting in slow growth. In order to continue growing at the right pace significant resources are necessary, which meant for most perfume and cosmetics firms at that time, the need to merge or sell. Other French brands had done so before.

When, because of my father's desire to retire and my brother embracing a political career, we decided to sell Orlane, there was no lack of offers, essentially from across the Atlantic, where we were already well known. We chose Norwich Products, which merged the same year with Morton International to create Morton-Norwich. The head office was in Chicago and as I became a member of its board of directors –Isabelle and I crossed the Atlantic several times a year, spending quite a lot of time in the US.

We lived our great American experience, a country which we loved and where we had a lot of friends. We kept our apartment in New York and got to know Chicago better, a superb city on the edge of Lake Michigan. The chairman of Morton-Norwich owned a house on the 30th floor of a building in the city, an authentic medieval castle, with its corner towers and a proper vegetable garden on the roof! In winter however, the icy north wind would sweep between the city's famous modern buildings and sometimes you had to hang on to the lampposts so as not to be blown away!

With Isabelle during a trip to the United States to promote Orlane.

In New York we had lots of friends and along with business we had quite a social life. We got to know some of New York's famous hostesses well and we would be caught up, for the short time we were there, in the social whirlwind of the moment. I recall some amusing anecdotes, such as the time when Isabelle, wearing trousers, was refused entry into the French restaurant, La Caravelle, very popular in those days. Like all the restaurants in the city back then, they did not allow trousers for women –so she went to the ladies room and returned wearing just her tunic and tights!

Another time, Isabelle, who had just had a cast removed from her broken leg, decided to wear white cotton knee-highs and accompanied me to the La Côte Basque restaurant. A reporter from Women's Wear Daily photographed her outfit. The following day, the photos were in the windows of Saks Fifth Avenue and the models were all wearing knee-high socks –it started a short-lived fashion trend. Americans are always on the lookout for new ideas –this is what makes this city so vibrant!

I was not happy with my father and my brother's decision to sell the family business –Jean d'Albret-Orlane –that we had founded and which was developing magnificently, but I did not have the financial means to buy them out. However, in the long run, this decision proved to be wise. My brother and I were both now married; our personal and family destinies would inevitably take different paths. This unavoidable and problem-free separation turned out to be a good thing. And here I was, the youngest of the three, ready to go my own way!

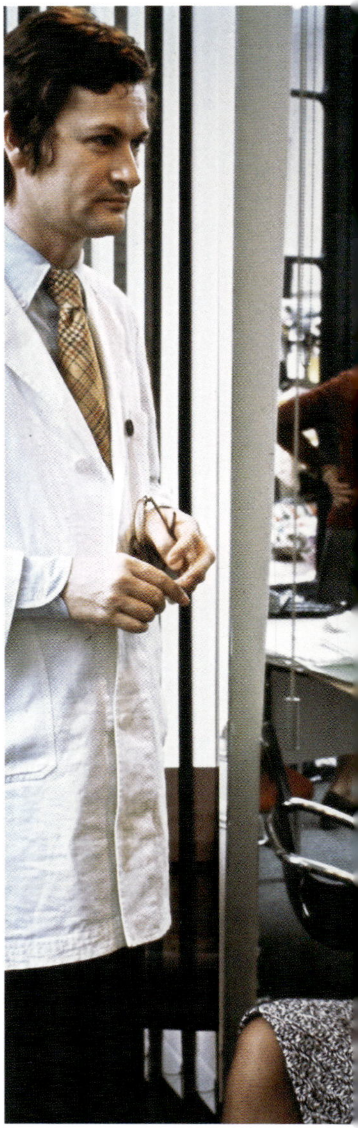

Isabelle and Jean-Louis Scherrer in the couture house workshops, Avenue Montaigne.

Becoming part of Morton-Norwich, while allowing Orlane to strengthen its overseas positions, changed nothing for the company that I was now running on my own. My father was honorary chair of the board of directors; I was CEO, and my brother retained the title of Technical Adviser. I was assisted by Gisèle Bidaud, the General Secretary in charge of financial matters, who had been by my side since 1953, and a team of close colleagues including Egmont Desperrois, Technical Director, Louis de Drouas, Industrial and Sales Director and Roland de Saint Vincent, Senior Vice President. Orlane continued growing in the wake of the incredible success of the B21 Cream. During the next five years the company, now an international group, doubled its sales figures.

In the 1970s the fashion designer Jean-Louis Scherrer, who was looking for financial backing, joined us. Orlane's strategy was to establish a new perfume department and Scherrer would bring the image of couture.

It was in 1971, whist I was dancing with Isabelle at the closing ball of the August Deauville season we saw Jean-Louis dancing with his wife, Laurence, whom we knew well. He came towards us and whispered in my ear,

"I've won my trial and have recovered my name..."
I replied straight off, "Come and see me tomorrow!"

Jean-Louis Scherrer, the quest for "universal femininity"

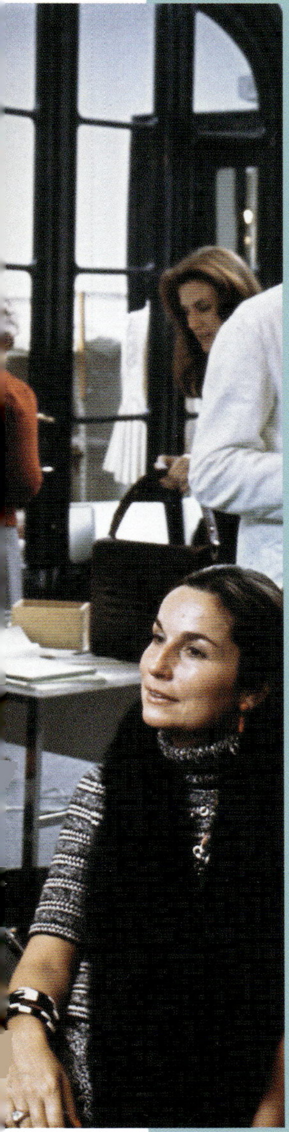

In the 1960s and 1970s, Jean-Louis Scherrer was one of the most promising figures in the Paris fashion world. The prestigious American department store Bergdorf Goodman signed an exclusivity contract with him, placing him on a par with Dior, Yves Saint-Laurent, Givenchy, etc. He trained at Christian Dior at the end of the 1950s, and then became a designer for Louis Féraud. Jean-Louis Scherrer opened his fashion boutique in 1962 at 182 rue du Faubourg Saint-Honoré. It was in this old wine cellar that he held his first ready-to-wear fashion show on January 30th 1963 to which Parisian high society and the fashion press rushed. He got first class reviews: his clothes were said to be fresh, distinctive, both sensual and vibrant: "I think women will always be feminine. Exacerbate this subtle femininity, it's beautiful!" said the man who had originally wanted to be a dancer.

The young designer's stylish and colourful clothes were worn by such clients as Michele Morgan, Françoise Sagan, Françoise Dorléac, the Empress of Iran Farah Diba, Baroness Von Thyssen, Mrs Patino later Paola of Belgium, Queen Noor of Jordan, Raquel Welch, Anemone Giscard d'Estaing, Isabelle Adjani, etc.

Jean-Louis Scherrer was Mme Valéry Giscard d'Estaing's preferred couturier. He designed her first official dress –a white bustier gown with discreet embroidery– which she wore to the reception held at Versailles in 1974 in honour of the Shah of Iran on his official visit to France. Never before that evening had a First Lady of France dared to show her shoulders!

However, in the interim he had clashed with his partner, the New York businessman Francis Francis, who wrongfully sold clothes produced by others under his label. Jean-Louis Scherrer managed to recover the use of what had become a brand and the young couturier was looking for a partner to start his own Haute Couture house. It would be Orlane.

With Isabelle, I got personally involved in the designer's fresh start. Jean-Louis Scherrer became a subsidiary of Orlane and we opened a series of ready-to-wear boutiques under his name. He joined The Chambre Syndicale de la Haute Couture, received the Haute Couture label, opened ten new stores, including one at 51 Avenue Montaigne in Paris, its new head office, and on the left bank 31 rue de Tournon. In 1974, Jean-Louis Scherrer became Couturier of the Year. Isabelle introduced him to the Kennedy family, giving him the opportunity to dress Jackie Kennedy and more particularly Pat Lawford, President Kennedy's sister, as well as his mother, Rose Kennedy. Consulted on each collection, Isabelle played the role of a precious and wise adviser to Jean-Louis Scherrer, thus assuring an essential link between the couturier and Orlane.

With Jean-Louis Scherrer now a part of Orlane, we had access to the aura that surrounds Haute Couture and all the benefits, often intangible, going well beyond the influence of a cosmetics brand. We intended to launch a perfume under his name, but ultimately it did not happen in our time. It was at Jean-Louis Scherrer that Isabelle first started working in the artistic and economic world of beauty.

When I finally left my executive position at Orlane, the management in Chicago did not wish to keep the couture house. Thanks to my efforts Jean-Louis recovered his house and name under excellent conditions, in 1976. From there he went on to develop his business and his name by himself throughout the 1980's with great success in the wake of the flagship store on Avenue Montaigne.

In 1974, I decided not to renew the seven-year contract that Morton-Norwich had offered me at that time. When I was with the Chicago group, I observed how they worked in the US and I adapted myself accordingly, I learned a lot about their way of management, which suited me perfectly. Americans take decisions and make them happen – they are comfortable in action. Bringing an idea to life calls for its immediate implementation. They are also very strict concerning the methods and regulations governing business. However, the freedom that was mine as head of the French company Orlane was being challenged with the arrival of new leaders –and changes in the top management in Chicago were becoming too frequent. So I left the company that I had co-founded with my brother. I continued as an adviser for one more year until the end of 1975.

At the beginning of 1976, I was free. Free to start yet another cosmetics adventure, this time with Isabelle.

At the beginning of the 1970s, in our apartment on Avenue Hoche.

Chapter 5

A new aventure, Sisley

“I love nature and the countryside, I am convinced that the scientific use of plant extracts have an extremely exciting future. In short, I believe in phytotherapy, Beauty from plants: a very innovative idea.”

Sisley is the name of a British impressionist painter, Alfred Sisley (1839-1899). It is also the name of the global brand that I developed with Isabelle. Two of my former colleagues, Roland de Saint-Vincent and Jean-François Laporte had chosen the name Sisley to start a small plant-based cosmetic business. Two years later they came to see me for financial assistance, which I gave willingly. However, in 1976, I bought back their shares. With my experience and my expertise in cosmetics, I made a new start.

"I did not start the Sisley adventure alone. My wife was by my side. Sisley was our common venture... our sixth child, we would say jokingly."

Begin a new business adventure at the age of fifty? Risk my personal fortune? In fact, since starting out on the roads of France after the war, I have always had in me the desire to embark on something new. I still remain inhabited by this entrepreneurial spirit that the family has had throughout the 20th century. Yet selling cosmetic products made from natural plant extracts in the crisis of the 1970s? There were very few who believed that such an idea had a future. My friends advised me against what they called "pure madness". One of my former suppliers at Orlane told me: "Go ahead, I admire you for it, but... I pity you." Well, we went ahead. One need not hope in order to undertake…

I did not start the Sisley adventure alone. My wife was by my side. Sisley was our common venture, our sixth child, we would say jokingly. Isabelle is an integral part of Sisley's creation and success. Symbolically, we interlaced the initials H and I inside the packaging of all Sisley products.

Isabelle

Drawing of Isabelle Potocka, by Ricardo Macarron.

Isabelle Potocka was seventeen when I first met her in Paris in the mid-1950s. Born in Poland, she grew up in Portugal and Spain, studied in England, started a family in France, developed an international business... like me, she is a citizen of the world. She speaks four languages fluently: Polish, French, Spanish and English; as well as a little Portuguese, the result of her family and personal history. A history that is by no means trivial, more like something out of a novel. Daughter of Joseph Potocki and Princess Christine Radziwill, Isabelle is a descendant of two of the most illustrious Polish families, the Potockis and the Radziwills.

The Potockis are an aristocratic Polish family whose roots can be traced back to the lordship of Potok, near Krakow, in the 12th century. Known for their statesmen, war chiefs and writers, the Potockis have left their mark on Polish history, where they once possessed immense estates in what is now the western part of Ukraine. Among them is Jan Potocki (1761-1815), the author of the Saragossa Manuscript, a major European work of literature. The Radziwills, for their part, are one of the most ancient and prestigious Lithuanian-Polish houses. Initially the Voivode of Vilnius, since 1518 its members have borne the title of Princes of the Germanic Roman Holy Empire bestowed on them by the Emperor Charles the Fifth.

When, in 1930, Joseph Potocki married Christine Radziwill, the Polish aristocracy was living its last carefree days. The occupation and division of Poland, the Second World War, and the establishment of communism were about to engulf their world. When the Second World War broke out, Isabelle's father was in the diplomatic service. His country had been invaded, was occupied, and he had to get to Romania with the Polish Foreign Office. His wife and his three

Helenka
1892

Above from left to right: Hélène and Joseph Potocki, Janusz and Anna Radziwill, the grand-parents of Isabelle; watercolours of the Potocki Palace on Avenue Krakowskie Przedmiescie in Warsaw and the Château of Nieborów; below from left to right: the Radziwill family at afternoon tea at Nieborów, before World War I; heading off for the hunt at Antoniny, the Potocki palace in Volhynia, today Ukraine; Joseph and Christine Potocki, Isabelle's parents, with the great pianist Arthur Rubinstein in Madrid.

daughters were deported with the Radziwill family to a Russian camp in Szepetowka, which happened to be located on Potocki land on the Polish-Soviet border. The castle had been destroyed in 1928, but the residents from the neighbouring village secretly brought them food and information during the night. Thankfully the King of Italy Victor-Emmanuel III and Count Ciano, Mussolini's son-in-law, who knew the family before the war, saw their names on a list of prisoners. With their intervention, the family was set free after a few months.

"Like many others, my mother-in-law's family would experience the dark times that Poland was going through at that time."

Like many others, my mother-in-law's family would experience the dark times that Poland was going through at that time. Prince Janusz Radziwill, Isabelle's grandfather, head of the Polish conservative party between the two world wars, had turned his home Nieborów, near Warsaw, into a very beautiful residence where celebrities and prominent politicians were entertained. In 1939, he was arrested for the first time and interrogated by the NKVD, the Soviet Secret Service. During the German occupation, he carried out clandestine activities and participated in the Warsaw Uprising from August 1st to October 2nd 1944, during which the Polish home army rose up against the German occupiers. During these two months, almost 200,000 people died and the city was totally destroyed.

Joseph and Christine Potocki.

Janusz Radziwill was imprisoned by the Nazis for a few months in Berlin, where he remained until December 1944. Upon his return, he was arrested again by the NKVD, sent to Moscow and interrogated in the Loubianka prison. Then from 1945 to 1949, he was imprisoned for three years in the Krasnogorsk camp, near Moscow with other members of his family. It was there that his wife Anna, née Princess Lubomirska, died and was buried in an anonymous tomb. Janusz Radziwill was able to return to Warsaw where he passed away in 1967, without ever returning to Nieborów.

Meanwhile, in the aftermath of the war and with the establishment of communism firmly taking hold, all property had been confiscated.

This included the Potocki Palace on Avenue Krakowskie Przedmiescie, in the centre of Warsaw, where my wife was born, which had been meticulously rebuilt after the war and converted into government offices. Today it is home to the Ministry of Culture.

Joseph Potocki, my future father-in-law, as I have mentioned, had left Poland with the Ministry of Foreign Affairs in September 1939. He was able to reach Rome where his family joined him, then France, before settling in Portugal, where he occupied the second and later the top post at the Polish Embassy, representing the Polish government exiled in London. He was also president of the Polish Red Cross.

The establishment of the People's Republic of Poland, headed by the Committee of Lublin created by Stalin, deprived the Polish government in London of any international recognition. Only two countries refused to recognise the new Polish communist government and continued to support the "free Poles", the Vatican and Spain. Joseph Potocki remained the Polish Plenipotentiary Minister and lived in exile in Spain from 1944 until his death in 1968. I remember my father-in-law being a very tall, elegant man with a lot of class, intelligent and ever at ease. My mother-in-law was a bright, beautiful and courageous woman, for whom I had boundless admiration.

In addition to Polish, my wife's second language is Portuguese. She lived in Estoril for four years with her parents before settling in Madrid. Isabelle grew up with her brother Peter and her two sisters Ann and Dorothy in Spain, which was then poor and drained as a result of the civil war. She was educated there and learned to speak perfect Spanish. She later acquired the Spanish nationality which she retained until our marriage. Every Christmas, and especially at Easter, the family continued to practice Polish customs, a tradition that we continue to this day with our children.

Even if she had lived almost her entire life outside Poland, Isabelle always felt Polish. During her trips and travels, she took great pleasure in meeting her fellow compatriots. After 1989 when democracy finally arrived in Poland, we got actively involved in the country's social, artistic and cultural life. However she still remains deeply attached to Spain, which had welcomed her family so warmly and where she had grown up happily with her sisters and her brother in Madrid. Two of them as well as one of our daughters Elisabeth, having married Spaniards, now live there.

Then one day Isabelle, age 17 met a young Frenchman called Hubert d'Ornano –who was also born in Poland– at a dinner organised by friends, Louis and Roselyne de Chollet, at the Automobile Club, Place de la Concorde. It was in 1955 and I remember I had just won the Grand Prix de Paris for Pigeon Shooting. She had come from Oxford for the weekend and was sitting next to me:
"I live in Spain, but I'm Polish," she said to me.

To her great surprise, I replied in Polish! From that day on, I sent her a card every year at Christmas. "The Frenchman hasn't forgotten you, once again he's sending you his season's greetings," her sisters would tease her.

Christine Potocka and the president John Kennedy at the baptism of Tina, Stas and Lee Radziwill's daughter.

Time passed, I saw Isabelle in London, where she worked and shared a flat with an American friend Jill Weldon. It was there that I met Stanislas Radziwill, her mother's younger brother. We became great friends and I often went shooting with him at Helmsley, one of the most beautiful shoots in England. An original and engaging personality, "Stas " as he was called, was a "grand seigneur". Having become a British subject, he was involved in the creation of the Sikorski Historical Institute in London and built St. Anne's church in remembrance of his mother, who had died in the Russian camp, at the Mercy school for Polish boys near Henley-on-Thames. Strangely enough I met Isabelle through Roselyne de Chollet, the first wife of Stas, who

Stas Radziwill, Isabelle's uncle, during a shoot at La Renaudière.

then married Grace Kolin and later Lee Bouvier, Jacqueline Kennedy's sister, now known as Lee Radziwill. In Chicago, Stas had actively supported his brother-in-law John Kennedy during the US presidential campaign in November 1960, which was a particularly close election. Indeed, only about 100,000 votes separated him from his rival Richard Nixon. That is why the day on which he took office in Washington, John Kennedy gave him his picture with these words on it, referring to Stas's campaign in Chicago in front of the Polish Americans:
"You've made it!"

Through Stas and Lee we would become friends with the Kennedy family some of whom we saw often during the 1960s. John Kennedy, of whom we caught a brief glimpse before his assassination in Dallas in November 1963, was an attractive and brilliant personality, eager to accomplish things, as if he were aware of the brevity of his destiny. Isabelle's parents visited Washington the week before his assassination. They saw the Presidential couple several times at the White House and even spent the last weekend with John and Jacqueline in Virginia before their fatal trip to Texas. My mother-in-law rode beautifully and enjoyed riding with Jackie.

However, I cannot speak of John Kennedy without mentioning his brother Bobby who was assassinated five years later, another equally exceptional personality. We had supper with him during his last stay in Paris, an evening that ended with a long walk along the river Seine between the Louvre and Alexandre III Bridge.

Getting back to courtship!

On each of my trips across the Channel, I always made a point of visiting Isabelle in London. I was at a shoot in Spain at Christmas in 1962 when she told me she was on her way to the United States. She was

Count Hubert d'Ornano (second from left) and his bride with the latter's uncle, Prince Stanislas Radziwill and Princess Radziwill, sister of America's First Lady, at the luncheon following the d'Ornano-Potocka rites in Deauville. Seeberger

D'Ornano-Potocka Marriage in France

going to be working at the Spanish Embassy in Washington for Antonio Garrigues y Díaz-Cañabate (1904-2004), a great lawyer, friend of her parents and new Spanish Ambassador to the US. He later became the Minister of Justice in the first government under King Juan Carlos I.
"I am leaving for the US for two years," she told me.

Our wedding at Deauville, July 6th 1963; flying off for our honeymoon immediately after.

At almost thirty-seven, I was a happy and accomplished bachelor. This unexpected announcement hit me right in the chest. I had to prevent Isabelle from moving to the other side of the Atlantic for two long years. Two days later, I proposed to her! For a d'Ornano, marrying Isabelle Potocka after my ancestor Marie Walewska and my mother Elisabeth was surely a quirk of fate! Isabelle later asked me, half-jokingly:
"When we met was it love at first sight or was it because I was born Polish?".

"Both," I replied smiling. But love comes from elsewhere...

After our engagement we were married a few months later in Deauville on July 6th 1963, first at the civil ceremony at the City Hall, then at the religious wedding at St Augustine's Church. The service was conducted by Father Alex-Cjeslas Rzewuski, a Dominican uncle of Isabelle's. He had been a well-known artist close to Jean Cocteau and Maritain, and later in life a French writer. Surrounded by his four deputies, my brother Michel, who had only been Mayor of Deauville for seven months, officiated at our civil union before joining the crowd of guests. So deeply

moved after we declared our mutual "Yes", he almost forgot to pronounce the established formula "By the power invested in me, I now pronounce you husband and wife" (which would have invalidated the civil union). Eight hundred guests had come from France and all over the world, a large number were relatives, friends and colleagues. A train was even reserved from Saint Lazare railway station in Paris with a hairdresser on board. Our wedding was described as "original, merry and elegant" by the press and a number of magazines.

Looking radiant and happy, Isabelle wore a dress by Jean Patou. Pope Paul VI sent his blessing. The soloists from the Paris Opera sang the Coronation Mass by Mozart, the music ringing out under the arches. The Gien hunting horns played "Les Honneurs" [The Honours] and "Le Salut à Saint Hubert" [Salute to St Hubert] as we left the church "to the cheers of the locals", as the newspaper reported.

A new life began for us. Firstly we thanked those to whom we owed our presence in the world. Isabelle's parents and my father were with us and, as we told a few friends and relatives: "Family means more than anything to us. Today, we remember my mother Elisabeth who would have been so happy to have shared this wonderful occasion with us."

From then on I built my family life and my life in general with Isabelle; together we created a unique business, Sisley.

Sisley

When I took over Sisley, I had almost thirty years of experience in cosmetics, and I had also started a few other small businesses on the side. In the 1960s, when we created Orlane, I devoted my free time to agriculture. I developed a successful business of unpasteurized milk in glass bottles sold in the Châteauroux region. The bottles ordered were delivered every morning to the customer's front door, just like in England. The success was however short-lived with the arrival of supermarkets selling milk in cartons. I also had a go at quails for a while! It started in an amusing way. Returning from Italy after a race in which I had run, someone offered me twenty live quails which I sent back with the race horses. I thus began a small breed. To help boost demand, I offered a few quails to restaurants around Châteauroux, which included them on their menus and because of the success, ordered more. This also lasted a few years!

“Sisley was a business we developed and it was entirely ours. I implemented the best of what I'd learned over the past decades, what my father had taught me and the family experience accumulated over two generations.”

I have always loved competition. I belonged to a football club that often played before the National French matches. During a stay in Saint Moritz, when I was still single, friends persuaded me to try bobsleighing. I loved to speed down the ice track in the Swiss resort. There was a good atmosphere. One day, an Englishman whom I did not know came to see me and asked if he could try the sport with me. He turned up at the appointed time. He had probably made a bet and had a few drinks before, to give himself courage. However, when I reached the bottom of the run, I turned around and my English teammate had disappeared... he had fallen off somewhere! We looked for him along the run but never found him! On a more serious note, I won an international competition before stopping after an accident: my bobsleigh crashed during a training session, my teammate ended up with a broken arm and I had a damaged neck.

With Isabelle in Sisley's offices, Avenue George V.

Sisley was a business we developed and it was entirely ours. I implemented the best of what I'd learned over the past decades, what my father had taught me and the family experience accumulated over two generations. I also wanted to build a French company that would be recognised worldwide. I do business out of duty and ambition and of course to make enough money to lead the life we wish to live. Aristocracy is no longer just a legacy or a belonging, it brings a responsibility to maintain and continue a heritage for our children through what we do and create today. In my case, I was never attracted by finance, I am an industrialist who seeks to build and produce and of course participate in our country's economy.

With Gisèle Bidaud, my long-time financial assistant who had returned to work with me, I established a four-year business and development plan. She provided invaluable assistance in structuring the first years of the company. As we expected, we invested for the first four years. We recovered our losses in the fifth year and for nineteen years we did not pay dividends, we reinvested all the profits in the business. Indeed, we started the business during the middle of the 1970s economic oil crisis, a bit like my father had done with Lancôme in the 1930s. The eight people with me, most of them former colleagues from Orlane who wished to continue working with me, moved into a few rooms on Avenue Mozart, before settling in a small office at 102, Avenue des Champs-Elysées. On the ground floor was the Turkish Tourist Office, hence the occasional bomb scare! The premises were cramped, space was limited, so much so that my colleagues would say jokingly that they did not dare to leave their seats for too long if they wanted to find them again!

With Isabelle, we were back on the road visiting our old clients, the perfumeries of Paris and France, to sell them our new products. Once again, we had to be persuasive, explain and convince them, as no one was waiting for us, the shelves of their shops were crowded with cosmetics of all kinds. In addition, the economic climate was not favourable.

Thus we organised a meeting in Bordeaux, with the president of the local perfumers. He warned us, "I will talk to my colleagues, but I'm afraid there won't be many of us tonight. And I don't think I can sell your cosmetics myself, even if they seem excellent."

First image of Sisley, which gives the tone of the new company and the new spirit of the brand; top right, Sisley's initial logo.

In fact that evening no one came, we were alone with him. But he was won over, and we persuaded him to become our exclusive

distributor for the largest city in the southwest of France! The same thing happened elsewhere. We organised dinners in all the cities where we wanted to sell our products and we invited the regional perfumers. The table was decorated with our personal tablecloths, dishes and the d'Ornano family silverware!
"Prepare dinner as we would do at home!" I said to Isabelle.

We gave a dinner in Cannes for the perfumers of the South of France. The dinner at the Moulin de Mougins was delicious and its decoration unique. The president of the perfumers of the South sat next to Isabelle. He too was totally won over and adopted our brand –just like most of the other guests.

Dine in your city with the d'Ornanos: the formula proved to be successful and widened our circle of clients, even if we had to pack and ship the silverware, etc. each time. In Lyon, Isabelle organised lunch at the famous Paul Bocuse –of course with all the d'Ornano decoration! Charmed by the beauty of the tables, Bocuse said a few words himself before lunch! We received the same encouraging welcome everywhere. In Lille, the owner of the largest perfumery in the city became one of our best clients and a personal friend. It has to be said that at that time these great perfumeries in the cities of France were true local institutions. Unfortunately, today they have been replaced by major perfumery chains.

Our business grew thanks to the quality and effectiveness of our products. From day one, those who tried adopted them straightaway. The fancy packaging would come later. In addition to advertising campaigns, samples are the best way to convince. Isabelle and I were full of energy and believed in our young enterprise. We were proud of the quality of our products and liked to share our enthusiasm and our convictions. We did things our way –we chose to do them differently.

SISLEY INTRODUCES PROTECTIVE FACE CARE

PHOTO BY STEVE FOXALL

Hubert and Isabelle d'Ornano

The d'Ornanos Hit Dallas

Sisley, which is sold in only 23 doors in the United States, has become the fastest-growing treatment line at Neiman Marcus, according to a spokesman for the store.

To promote the line, Count Hubert and Countess Isabelle d'Ornano — who founded Sisley — have been making store appearances in the United States, including a recent stop at the Neiman Marcus flagship in downtown Dallas.

Sisley, which is sold exclusively in the U.S. at Neiman Marcus and Bergdorf Goodman, was founded in 1974. The company bases its products on botanical ingredients, including extracts from vegetables, plants, fruits, flowers and herbs. Prices range from $18 for a lipstick to $175 for 1 ounce of the company's Sero Botanique, an intensive treatment lotion for the face and body.

During their appearance in Dallas, the d'Ornanos said sales for the skin care line were far exceeding expectations.

"Last month our sales were up 50 percent in France. The forecast was 20 percent," said Hubert d'Ornano, who co-founded Orlane Beauty Products in 1946. His father started Lancome.

"We are also doing especially well in Japan, which is our first country of exportation," he added.

The d'Ornanos plan to launch Eau de Soir, the company's first women's scent, in August. Eau de Campagne, for both sexes, was launched in 1977 and is the company's only other scent.

"We discovered the restorative benefits of natural products through our research laboratories," said Isabelle d'Ornano, artistic director of Sisley. "We spend from 7 percent to 10 percent on research. This is the basis of our business."

Sisley's new eye shadow line has been a breakthrough for the company, she said.

"Until now, we have not offered an eye shadow," she said. "This was because we knew of no way to extract lasting colors directly from plants and vegetables. We've recently discovered a way to preserve such colors, and we now offer treatment eye shadows."

According to the Neiman Marcus spokesman, the Sisley line is among the most expensive offered at the store.

"Sales are doing very well," the spokesman said. "We're running double-digit figures ahead of last year."

COMTESSE HUBERT D'ORNANO

Administrateur chez Sisley

« Cela pourrait s'appeler l'habitude, la tradition, ou la mémoire : ce sac en résille d'or, ma mère et ma grand-mère le portaient déjà. »

"Call it habit, tradition or sentiment: this gold mesh bag was used by my mother and my grandmother."

Page 8

Two Paris Women

By Hebe Dorsey

PARIS, Oct. 29 (IHT) — In the deceptively frivolous beauty business, the image is at least as important as the bottle content. The success of such firms as Helena Rubinstein, Elizabeth Arden and now Estee Lauder was heavily rooted into those women's strong, not to say overpowering, personalities as well as their competence and go.

Two women, both prominent Parisian figures, are joining the club with the hope that their beautiful image will influence women at the beauty counter. One is Helene Rochas, the other is Isabelle d'Ornano.

The late Helena Rubinstein, her jewels, her art collection, her lifestyle, was a legend in her own time. Then, there were all those clever little stories of how she concocted that magic cream on a back burner, a secret passed on by generations of

Challengers

Botanical beauty line flowers

Nobility's doing a bloomin' business at Neiman-Marcus

By Lynn Berk
SUN Staff Writer

In the beginning plants just looked pretty.

Flourishing in the wilds or scrambling for survival in somebody's stone pot, their only known function was to add a spot of color to an otherwise drab and colorless cave. (Neanderthals did not know a great deal about photosynthesis).

Then somebody discovered that besides looking pretty, certain plants could cure colds or shrink warts or cool burns so moms everywhere, even ancient ones, forced ailing kids to drink concoctions that looked bad and tasted worse.

On to the 20th century, when somebody else figured out plants would do better if we hold conversations with them (wouldn't we all?). In California they've taken to munching on them. Sisley beauty products made with the extract of plants as common as sage, orange blossoms, lilies and cucumbers.

In the olden days titles were given along with the money and land courtesy of the king. Titles are still given, but the money and land is omitted and people like Count Hubert and Countess Isabelle d'Ornano, as he himself genially admits, have to work for a living.

Chances are they would work anyway. They are both bright, ambitious people; she is consistently on the world's best-dressed list, he a member of France's oldest aristocracy. Although they live in Paris and have an 18th-century country house they have gone back to the earth for this line of beauty care that uses roses as tonics, lime to relieve congestion, hops and soya to fight wrinkles and woodmallow to soften and moisturize. Sisley Countess Isabelle does the marketing and public relations for the company and she also does most of the talking, explaining that she and her husband believe the future of beauty care lies in plant extracts.

"We believe a line based on natural products, rather than synthetics, would have an enormous future," she said, and he added that future has been bolstered with the use of highly technical equipment that now makes such extracts both visible and accessible.

"We buy these extracts from all over the world," he said, "From Asia, Germany, the United States and France. Fifteen years from now all cosmetics will be made with plant extracts," and, Countess Isabelle continued, "We believe nature has everything man needs. Before, there was no way to find that our. Now there is scientific proof and there are far women the world over are co cerned about.

"She might have a particul problem, but mostly she wants stop aging and to keep the skin good condition. They can all hav beautiful skin, they can all have glow. Lines and wrinkles are expression of life, of what y have and what you have not, a there is nothing that will ta them away once they are there

"But women can glow. That what they can do."

She won't come out and co demn those products tha purportedly make those line vanish, but she does say, "If yo use something early enough yo will still get them, but later. Onc you have them, they're there."

He reaches over to caress t few lines that crinkle her eyes ar dimple her face. "Some wrinkles he said, "are quite charming. Ta them out and you lose a lot of you personality."

The Countess of cosmetics

BY ANTHEA HALL

WHEN Isabelle d'Ornano first visited the country seat of her husband's family, she was surprised to find that there was a nearby forest called after the famous cosmetic firm: *la forêt de Lancôme.*

Of course it was a silly mistake on her part. The reverse was the case. The d'Ornanos called their first cosmetic firm after the forest; their second was a word play on the name Ornano with two letters changed: Orlane. To complete the hat-trick, their third is called Sisley.

Sisley — doesn't the word have a certain franglais-like thud about it (would General de Gaulle have approved?)? Or does it conjure up Impressionist landscapes, green and peaceful?

"Anyway, it sounds well in all languages," said Isabelle, Comtesse d'Ornano who, being Polish-born, brought up in Portugal and Spain, having worked in England and married in France, should certainly know. She tried it in five languages: "Sisley, Sisley, Sisley, Sisley, Sisley—I don't think I can say it any

Isabelle d'Ornano: Sisley in five languages.

pal plant ingredients sound like a health food restaurant menu: avocado, calendula, grapefruit, ginseng, tomato, wheat germ, soya, sage. "And

what they needed was a very exclusive, expensive line which would export well. You can sell cheap products in your own country but not

also a renowned hostess at he parties in their apartment o the Quai d'Orsay in Paris.

But just how does someon who doesn't like dinne parties, can't stand going t bed late and hates being pi ned down, manage to becom a great hostess?

It is quite simple. She ha invented a new kind of pai less party.

All you do is to invit about 140 people round ever three months or so to a buff and call it "open house which means, apparently, th you can stay just a quarter an hour or the whole evenin until midnight.

Here is the d'Ornano theor of entertaining in full: " like seeing people—but seein a lot of people—and mixin people, which is difficult if yo sit them down (I only like si ting down to dinner with re friends).

"You don't have to wor about shy people who mig find it difficult if there we only about 40 people; but wi 150 it's like a stage or a spe tacle where they can wa around and not talk to an body and have their dinner

INTERNATIONAL HERALD TRIB

ty Business

allenging Big-Name Firms

Hebe Dorsey

ochas (left), Isabelle d'Ornano.

the president was a frequent guest at the d'Ornanos' exquisitely Proustian, 15-room apartment overlooking the Seine, where the mementos include a 16th-century portrait of a Polish queen. "One of my distant ancestors," the Polish-born countess said. All that and five children, plus a cosmetics company they started five years ago, give the d'Ornanos a rich life.

The d'Ornanos are not exactly new to the cosmetics business as the count, 46, will have you note. His father founded Lancome and Orlane and the latter purchased the fashion house of Jean Louis Scherrer. After his father sold Orlane, count Hubert opened his own house in 1974 and put his wife on his board of directors to advise on advertising, publicity, displays, promotion and packaging — "all of which is very feminine," he said.

e Madame Rochas, who ad-
at despite her joining the
e is very much on the out-

From the outset, the American press, like The International Herald Tribune, Women's Wear Daily, Town & Country *took an interest in us and our natural, high-quality approach which was much appreciated and personified our products. They quoted us and praised Isabelle, "the active Paris Woman", devoting precious articles to the lady they called the "Countess of Cosmetics" and her "French Touch".*

The same happened abroad where we drew on our past experience, as well as our friends and the network of contacts that we had already built. I knew the French and European markets very well, especially the Italian market as it is a country that is important for cosmetics and one we love. Italy immediately became our first foreign market. Isabelle, on the other hand, grew up in an international environment in which she was at ease. The fact that she worked in fashion at Jean-Louis Scherrer helped us since she got to know the major magazines and journalists very well. England, Spain, America, the department stores and all the international brands that matter in the world, held few secrets for us.

In 1981, we legally established our first subsidiary outside France, in Germany. It rapidly became operational. Indeed, it is essential to control the image and the way in which our luxury brand is being distributed. So rather than using a distributor, we created our own local subsidiary to develop Sisley, we chose the best outlets, and invested in building brand awareness.

Elsewhere though, we sometimes decided to use exclusive distributors. In Canada, we knew the family that founded the Holt Renfrew department stores. Its president, and a member of the founding family, Mr Shavik, came to Paris for the ready-to-wear collections. He bumped into Isabelle on Avenue Montaigne. She mentioned to him that we had started a new business.
"So what are you doing now?" he asked her.
"We are in the process of launching a line of high

quality beauty products based on plant-derived ingredients."

His reply was immediate:
"I want them in our stores!"

The reaction was the same sometime later at Bergdorf Goodman in New York, where Ira Neimark, the president, wanted the brand exclusively.

With Isabelle in the United States, in the 1970s, to promote the new cosmetics brand, Sisley.

We also enjoyed a lasting friendship with John Fairchild, the undisputed head of Women's Wear Daily for decades. He was the dreaded judge of fashion collections in France and Italy, and a legendary figure for his judgments, whatever the reputation of those covered by his magazine. He and his wife, Jill, remained close friends. Shirley Lord, editor of the beauty pages of *Harper's Bazaar*, and later *American Vogue* for a number of years also helped us with her articles supporting Sisley. She was married to Abe Rosenthal, the brilliant journalist who created the *New York Times Magazine* and whom we liked very much. Shirley Lord has published several "bibles" on health and beauty in the US. Carrie Donovan, another great journalist for the *New York Times Magazine*, in charge of the "Art of Living, Fashion and Beauty" section, also helped us. She regularly sent her magazine to Isabelle and would have lunch with her during Paris fashion week, asking her opinion.

We were helped by leading New York figures such as Diana Vreeland who was a very original and incomparable personality. She made *Harper's Bazaar* a success before the war and was editor-in-chief of *Vogue USA* when we met her in New York at Stas and Lee Radziwill's home. She had an exceptional instinct for what

Americans call "style". During her trips to Paris, she regularly had lunch with us at our home, along the Quai d'Orsay; I think she liked our apartment –she fitted in well! Diana Vreeland launched and worked with the greatest photographers. Her alter ego at Condé Nast, with an equally exceptional personality, was Alex Liberman, Russian by birth, editor, painter, photographer, sculptor; he was the artistic soul of Condé Nast for decades. His second wife Tatiana du Plessix Liberman, herself Russian, possessed a hypnotic personality. One of the great Russian poet Mayakovski's muses in the 1920s, she became a New York fashion icon after 1945, and the well-known hat designer for Saks Fifth Avenue for twenty years. We enjoyed entertaining Alex and Tatiana often in Paris.

"I like to invent the best possible products, not yet available on the market! We work in our own way, without copying anyone. I forbid that the names of our competitors and other products be mentioned. Why give them undue publicity?!"

Isabelle and I were very much involved in developing the US market with which we were familiar, and aware of just how important it was. We recruited and trained Francette Léguillon, who became a loyal and precious manager over there. Twice a year we visited our counters in the speciality stores that had requested, and been granted, exclusivity. The high costs involved in accessing the North American market, USA and Canada, drove us to develop an original approach which involved delivering our products directly to the stores, from France, just as if they were French clients. We were able to apply this approach, which avoided stock and distributors, because on both sides of the Atlantic we were looking for exclusivity in the best stores. The North American market was profitable for Sisley from day one. I remember the time we offered breakfast in a cosmetics department to all the sales people in Dallas. With the help of Isabelle I served coffee and tea. The staff present was delighted and it gave us the opportunity of getting to know those who sell our products as well as leaving us with some great memories. We did this quite often during our trips to the stores! Isabelle is a modern woman, capable of talking about "Sisley in four different languages", and who can speak about the skin with French, American and Latin women; discuss how to put their makeup on, and how to dress. The fact that Sisley is easily pronounced in most languages and that our brand was registered worldwide would greatly simplify things. The press was interested by my wife's history, particularly as she embodied the art of living and being of a French woman.

Our first years were promising. In 1981, we left our cramped quarters on the Champs-Elysées for the 2nd and 6th floors at 16 avenue George V, our current address, where we gradually occupied the entire building. Sisley was steadily growing around three fundamental principles: entrepreneurship, quality and innovation.

"We are and I hope we will remain a family business because we do not need the stock markets to help us grow. This independence has given us the time to build a global brand, without looking for a quick return on investment. But it also came at a price: as I have already said, for almost twenty years, all our profits were reinvested in the development of the company."

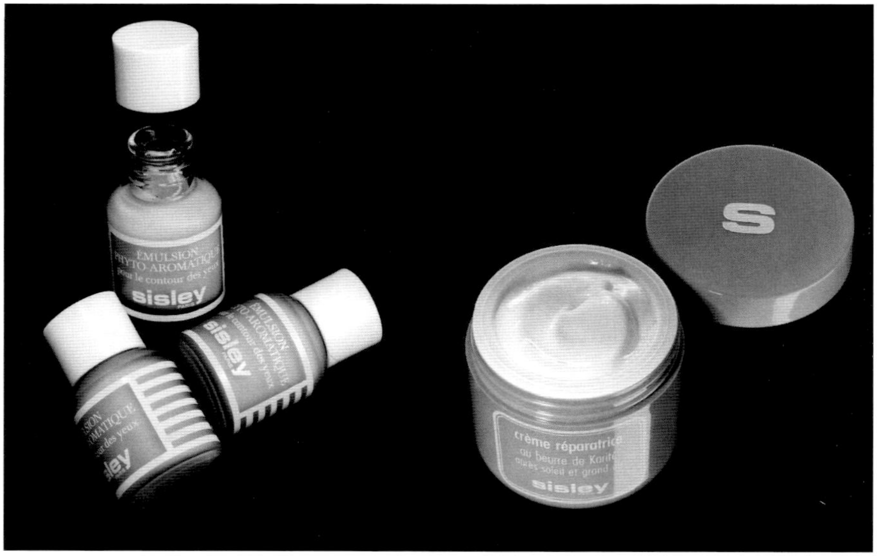

Some Sisley products as they looked back in the 1980s!

Entrepreneurship comes first. I am a businessman, a man who knows exactly where he is going, who likes to create and develop. We are, and I hope we will remain, a family business because we do not need the stock markets to help us grow. This independence has given us the time to build a global brand, without looking for a quick return on investment. But it also came at a price: as I have already said, for almost twenty years, all our profits were reinvested in the development of the company.

A company is built with others. Initiative and a sense of responsibility cannot be developed alone. I like to create with a team. I trust, I delegate and I like everyone to prove themselves and develop their talents. My door is always open, as you have to work with others, talk with everyone and be very approachable, in Paris as well as abroad. Probably a legacy of our Catholic education, we believe that people come before business. If those who work with us are not happy in their job, what we do is meaningless, an ideal which of course we manage to achieve more or less well. But as Sisley has developed, I am glad to see that those who have joined us have tended to stay and flourish. When some of my children started working for Sisley, I would never order them around. Instead I would guide, advise and encourage them, training them in the field and helping them to solve problems by themselves.

Second comes quality. I am intuitive, a creator, a pioneer, but also a developer. Many people have ideas, but making them happen is a completely different matter. Technology and research are only meaningful if they lead to effective creations, which meet the specific needs of our consumers and the high standards we have established. I go straight to the point, and I like to achieve the goals I have set. The strength of our family business lies in the fact that decisions can be made quickly. I like to invent the best possible products, not yet available on the market! We work in our own way, without copying anyone. I forbid that the names of our competitors and other products be mentioned. Why give them undue publicity?!

And thirdly innovation. Isabelle and I constantly test, stimulate, and push our chemists to their limits so that they develop new and better skincare and makeup formulas. With no limit of cost or time, our chemists are given great freedom in their work so that they can formulate unique products in the best possible conditions. The objective is twofold: a product is only launched once it has been perfectly achieved and does not need to be constantly reformulated.

All our existing products are selling very well, but over the years, we have thus created a series of "cult products", many of which still continue to be best sellers. The Emulsion Ecologique, the Crème Réparatrice, Sisleÿa, as well as Eau du Soir have loyal customers, and gain new followers every year through word of mouth. That is the way the reputation of a brand is established. Consumer confidence, once achieved, must be maintained.

Extract from a story by Madame Figaro *on Sisley's style.*

Emulsion Ecologique.
Chaque jour, matin et soir, et
vous verrez la différence.
Une formule ultra-légère, non grasse, immédiatement absorbée, à utiliser seule ou sous tout autre produit de soin Sisley, quel que soit le type de peau. Ce complexe synergique de nombreux extraits naturels de plantes - dont Centella Asiatica et Ginseng - protège la peau de toute pollution ambiante, améliore l'élasticité, donne de l'éclat. Il revitalise et hydrate* efficacement. Résultat : un teint lumineux, une peau plus lisse, plus souple, une apparence plus tonique.
* Les couches supérieures de l'épiderme.
Flacon verre 125 ml. Taille voyage en plastique 50 ml.
sisley
PARIS
jour et nuit - day and night
sisley PARIS
émulsion écologique
ecological compound
4.2 FL OZ 125 ml
Faure Vadon Forest

Chapter 6

Plants are the petrol of the future

Over the years, our daughter Elisabeth has lent her face to the brand and products of Sisley.

“Over the years, I have realised that, modern technology will enable us to use the best of plant extracts, both for medicine and cosmetics. I love nature; I manage a forest, I have raised horses and at one time even dairy cows.”

As a Harvard professor said in the Seventies "plants are the petrol of the future". Over the years, I have realised that modern technology will enable us to use the best of plant extracts, both for medicine and cosmetics. I love nature; I manage a forest, I have raised horses and at one time even dairy cows! Awarded the Order of Agricultural Merit, I have always been close to the land and Isabelle shares my feelings. She believes in natural medicine; her mother treated her children with homeopathy, an approach that always pleased her.

Emulsion Ecologique, whose formula has remained unchanged over the last three decades, was the first bestseller from Sisley.

With my past experience in cosmetic research, I was convinced that the scientific use of natural plant extracts had a promising future. I believed in plant based cosmetics at a time when hardly anyone was familiar with the term. It was not only out of concern for the environment and ecology, although these matters are also very important to me, it is just that these new ingredients yield excellent results and are well tolerated when chosen well and combined in sophisticated formulas. In short, they opened up tremendous opportunities to meet skincare needs. The exclusive use of plants in a cosmetic line was a new idea at that time.

The best of plants…

My experience in cosmetics and my interest in new technologies in my field led me to regularly monitor new ingredients as they appeared. After the Second World War, the discovery of the electronic microscope, and the advances in extraction techniques enabled active ingredients produced by green chemistry to be isolated and studied scientifically. Our first results were very exciting; I could see an immense field of discovery that could be put to good use in producing effective cosmetic formulas. Nature gave us many particularly interesting ingredients, it gradually became easier to identify them and extract them scientifically.

We would make cosmetics differently. In 1976, phytotherapy, the science of extracting and conserving natural plant extracts and essential oils was still very new. That didn't matter. To increase our line of products, which was about a dozen at first, I called on Egmont Desperrois, the former head of R & D at Orlane, President of the World Society of Cosmetology and a leader in his field, then retired. We rebuilt and improved the existing line; we went in search of new formulas, of which Emulsion Ecologique would be the first. Very quickly, I invested in a small phytocosmetics research laboratory in Gennevilliers, in the north-west outskirts of Paris. The building served as a production line, packaging plant and logistics platform.

The objective of our research was to identify molecules from the plant world similar to those in the animal world, then extract the very best from the plant fibres. A single cream, like Sisleÿa Global Anti-Âge, contains up to fifty main active ingredients. The amount of synthetic preservatives is also limited as much as possible through the use of essential oils. It was not about following some trend, but identifying and using the most promising ingredients. Plants from all over the world, Asia, the USA, Germany and France to name a few... were harvested when their qualities were at their finest, extracted using the most suitable method to maintain effectiveness. We were not looking for exoticism at any cost, but the best synergy and dosage for the best possible result.

Our weekly meeting on Wednesday mornings with our scientific team became a ritual at Gennevilliers. On the way, with Isabelle, we always stopped at a café near the Place de l'Etoile, for our traditional cappuccino! No marketing plan or technical specifications, too intellectual for us. Again, I am an intuitive who loves to attain my goal, that is, products to serve the unspoken expectations of our future clients. Creams that moisturize, protect and regenerate the skin; cosmetics, with a soft, smooth, non-greasy texture which offer natural, unpretentious pleasure, no unnecessary frills.

Isabelle and I are very demanding but agree on the need for simplicity. A privilege of her education and the distinction that her family has always preserved and passed on during difficult times, she strikes all those around her with her naturalness and poise. Mother of five children, working woman, accomplished hostess, Isabelle is athletic –she loves to ski, swim, ride and play golf. Walking and gymnastics are part of her daily routine to stay in shape.

> *“Sisley is based on this creed: naturalness, simplicity, quality and balance...”*

Her natural simplicity as a modern, accomplished woman makes her Sisley's number one customer and consumer. She tries all the products that other women will later use regularly. Isabelle is the true face of the brand we created. “I am a woman who likes to be and feel natural. First and foremost, you wear makeup to feel good, that's why I don't like to put too much on. A healthy body and skin are very important. As a young girl, my mother taught me that it was essential to take care of my skin, and to do so as naturally as possible. Along with a healthy lifestyle and a healthy, balanced diet, your skin must be looked after, nourished, moisturized and protected, hence the importance I attach to the products that I use and their quality. Today, there is no excuse for not having beautiful skin. It is a state of mind that helps improve our beauty, our morale, our deepest being. My husband likes to say, “There are no ugly women anymore, only those who don't know how to be beautiful.”

Sisley is based on this creed: naturalness, simplicity, quality and balance. Presentations and publicity –limited, given our means at the beginning– were no substitute for the intrinsic quality of the product itself and the trust it must inspire in the consumer who purchases and uses it. It is the quality of a Sisley product and its ensuing result, not the packaging or the publicity, that will make a woman appreciate it and buy it again. This does, however, come at a price.

One day when the President of France asked Isabelle a little ironically "How is Hubert's new business doing?" she replied: "Mr President, I believe that what we do is by no means insignificant. It's incredible how important a good product can be for a woman. If governing means finding ways to make people happy, then cosmetics can play an important role, enabling women to feel good and be happier, and consequently their husbands and companions as well. This is good for the nation's morale!"

The President was a little surprised, but he could find absolutely no reply to such a message of common sense! Later, every time we met him, he never missed an opportunity to refer to our brand's success!

…to create the best cosmetics

As I already mentioned, Sisley began with about ten references which we enhanced and developed around a short product range, with simple packaging, focusing on plants and nature. Then we began to develop cult products, ahead of their time, poised for a long life and which remain bestsellers today.

The first one was Emulsion Ecologique, which we launched in 1980. Never reformulated, never repackaged (with the exception of the measuring cap), this comfortable, light cream, a synergistic complex of plants, was developed to help protect the skin from pollution and external aggressions. An adjective –"ecological"– which has become very popular, a visionary idea, a product that became widely successful and is still so today. Emulsion Ecologique is today one of Sisley's top ten best-selling products! Why this long term success? It is used by women –and increasingly appreciated by men– and its qualities, along with its superb texture and fragrance, protect and restore the skin's balance. Ecological ahead of its time, and so it still remains!

In 1989, we launched another bestseller: Crème Réparatrice au Beurre de Karité [or Crème Réparatrice with Shea Butter]. As its name indicates, it calms, soothes, relieves and repairs sores or cracks, skin damaged by the cold, wind and sun. The same year, Phytobust ultra light intensive firming treatment for the bust, rich in plant extracts and algae, horsetail, fucus, ivy, red vine, helps the skin regain elasticity and tone.

In 1990, Sisley struck gold again when it launched the Super Crème Solaire Visage, providing effective protection from the sun's rays which although essential for life, are one of skin's worst enemies. It was the first sunscreen to combine sun protection with the benefits of a treatment day cream. A true anti-aging sunscreen, it was also four times more expensive than the competition. It didn't matter; we openly launched the product with the simple slogan "the most expensive sunscreen in the world". The customer was thus aware beforehand of its unusual price for a sunscreen, but not for a day cream. Our reasoning was simple:
"Why do women use expensive and sophisticated cosmetics all year long yet settle for a basic sunscreen?"

The Super Crème Solaire Visage,
"the most expensive sunscreen in the world",
unveils a bronzing treatment cream,
an unheard of concept, despite the dangers
the sun represents to the skin.

L'Eau de Campagne, our first eau de toilette, expressing the approach and the attachment to nature which is the philosophy of Sisley.

Together with its sunscreen action, the original formula of the Super Crème Solaire helped strengthen the skin's natural photo-protective properties and it was also a skincare cream in its own right, hence its unwavering success.

From 1976 onwards, we grew rapidly and introduced also a line of treatment makeup, using the plant world to combine makeup with real skincare benefits. All formulas used in this makeup carry plant extracts with properties to protect the most sensitive areas of the face. We called it Phyto Maquillage Traitant, or Botanical Make-up.

There is no cosmetics brand without a perfume range. In 1976, we launched Eau de Campagne, a name which conveyed our approach and attachment to nature. This very modern fragrance was created by the then young "nose" Jean-Claude Ellena. It surprised people and immediately made headlines. The press and the "connoisseurs" loved it. Playing on the alchemy of contrasts, its scent is based on a combination of green tomato leaves, its dominant note, with fruit and flower extracts, jasmine, geranium, vetiver, etc. which give it a particularly original, fresh, tonic and elegant fragrance bringing back the glory of freshly cut grass. The packaging is inspired by a Radziwill ex-libris, and photos of our country home on the advertisement assert its difference. The whole Eau de Campagne line: bath oil, shower gel, deodorant, soap and home fragrance, bears the same look. Eau de Campagne is a reflection of Sisley, a high quality eau de toilette with character, that is fresh, original, timeless, pleasing to both women and men. It was designed in our image; it is Sisley and has become a classic.

Sisley follows its own path. In the mid-1990s, we refused the trend of exfoliating fruit acids because we considered they were harsh for the skin. At the time, these were best sellers and our sales suffered.

Ten years later, fruit acids had disappeared from most formulas. Going against the tide, we preferred to launch a moisturizing mask, Hydra Flash, with new ingredients that help improve cell cohesion and retain moisture in the skin. Sesame and rice extracts provide phytoceramides, in particular serine (a natural beta hydroxyl acid). Soft and smooth, Hydra Flash still has its followers worldwide.

In 1989, Eau du Soir was created for Isabelle, thirteen years after Eau de Campagne, as a souvenir of the Andalusian gardens of her childhood in Spain. In the evenings, as the sun sets, the philadelphus (sort of orange blossom), exhales its bewitching perfume. My wife wore it for two years before it became Sisley's second perfume. Its beautifully rich fragrant floral heart, combines philadelphus, rose, jasmine, lily and ylang ylang. Eau du Soir, an elegant floral-cyprus perfume, became an instant success and won several international fragrance awards. From 1998, the cap featured the face of a cosmic woman designed by the Polish sculptor Bronislas Krzysztof. We have known and loved his work for many years and during one of his visits to Paris we asked him:
"Bronek, would you design a sculpture that could be used as a cap for a perfume bottle?"
"Why not, I'll try, but only if I like the perfume!"

"A single cream, like Sisleÿa Global Anti-Âge, contains up to fifty main active ingredients. The amount of synthetic preservatives is also limited as much as possible through the use of essential oils."

Bronislas Krzysztof adored Eau du Soir and created about a dozen miniature sculptures for us. We chose two of them, one for Eau du Soir, and another when we launched Soir de Lune. Eau du Soir and its beautiful bottle have become a classic, and every year we have created a different limited edition for Christmas.

Other bestsellers were to come. In 1999, after ten years of development we launched Sisleÿa Global Anti-Âge –even our children used to say that it was our prototype which we would continue to improve but never launch. It is an outstanding anti-aging cream,

rich in active ingredients; the result of our desire to create an all-in-one product. It was developed ideally to fight, in one single product, all the effects of aging. Sisleÿa Global Anti-Âge is an anti-wrinkle, firming, moisturizing and anti-radical cream. Sisleÿa became a bestseller overnight in France and abroad: 100,000 jars were sold in less than six months, millions today. This unprecedented success led us to create Sisleÿa Eye Contour, Sisleÿa Elixir, Sisleÿa Extra-Riche for dry skin and Sisleÿa hand care cream. The name came to us when coming back from a meeting in Gennevilliers, crossing the Alma Bridge:
"We believe in its success, we'll call it simply Sisleÿa!"

For the first time we were linking the name of one our products to the name of the brand. Sisleÿa was expensive –1,250 francs (about €190). "People would buy it once, but not twice if they were not totally satisfied," Isabelle said. But many of our clients told our sales force, in France and abroad, that they had tried so many other creams, before always coming back to Sisleÿa. This is our philosophy –the price of our product reflects the effort that we put into the formula and the ingredients.

One day, during a research meeting, we had come to the end of the process for one of our new, but very expensive products, and our head chemist said grimly, "This product will prove unsellable because of its price. We've wasted five years of work."
I replied, "You have successfully developed the product I wanted. Don't worry about the price, that's my concern!"

Direct dialogue between the owners, Isabelle and I, and the chemists working for the company, was very rare in the world of cosmetics. We do not launch a product until we have found what we are looking for. We alone decide whether a product is ready to be launched or not, and if its quality justifies the price.

EAU DU SOIR
EAU DE PARFUM.
EAU
DU
SOIR
eau de parfum
Création
Hubert Isabelle d'Ornano
pour Sisley.
sisley
PARIS

L'Eau du Soir, a perfume reminiscent of Isabelle's Spanish childhood, featuring a cap representing the face of a cosmic woman by the Polish sculptor Bronislaw Krzysztof.

This demand for quality must be accompanied by quality service too. You have to sell the right product to each customer. We attach great importance to the recruitment and training of our sales people as our products must be presented carefully, and in an uncomplicated way by professionals who have a real understanding of our clients and their needs. From the start, we bring them together at seminars always held in the best hotels, where they also stay for the night. They sell our luxury products and they deserve to be treated like princesses!

A certain desire for style...

I like the words of Kipling who said that power should be mixed with a little character in order to seduce. Sisley has a certain style, an approach which has given it from the start its unique character. Isabelle is no stranger to this style. She is Sisley's first ambassador, in touch with our staff, our clients and our customers, and she has managed to represent, but also express and develop this style. She and her team supervise the thousand and one details, which combined, give a product its character: visuals, packaging, advertising, etc. I designed with her the brand's logo, recognisable at first glance, and a few years later the white and silver (or gold) packaging of our products.

My wife, Artistic Director of Sisley, and I, are responsible for the visual look of our brand. Over the years, Isabelle has played an increasingly important part in Sisley, participating in the Wednesday lab meetings and in the products and perfumes she was the first to try, test, and wear. She is thus actively involved with our chemists and me in the creation of new products.

Isabelle is the guardian of this Sisley style she created. It is first of all reflected in the places where we have lived, because our life is a whole and we do not like to separate our way of life from our business. We have entertained a lot in Paris and in our country home. We love our guests to mingle and meet, more or less informally, always encouraging stimulating conversations. My wife likes to say that what makes a successful dinner party is the mixture of guests from different backgrounds, different generations, friends old and new. It is quite unusual in France where social life is very formal.

"Sisley has a certain style, an approach which has given it from the start its unique character."

Eau de Campagne captures and shares our country home, our love of plants and nature. Eau du Soir is the apartment on Quai d'Orsay that we have had since 1974 and which we have decorated in our own taste with the help of Henri Samuel, the great decorator of his time, whom Jackie Kennedy had chosen to redecorate the rooms in the White House. From the start, we entertained family and guests, as well as clients and journalists at our home, and we still do. Built in the Louis XIV style in 1920, at the time of the International Exhibition in Paris, our building along Quai d'Orsay is a privileged meeting place.

We have created a home which truly reflects us, with a mixture of styles and periods, having chosen personally the fabrics, furniture, rugs, books, old and contemporary works of art. It has constantly evolved over the past two decades with undoubtedly more contemporary art now!

Isabelle loves to say, "When it is beautiful, everything goes together".

Art is an essential part of our life; we love being surrounded by beauty. We are not motivated by the desire to collect or to own, we personally choose each object for our homes, whether at a sale, at an artist's studio or in a gallery, provided that the object "speaks" to us, fits in with the spirit of the place, and inspires us. We continue to buy and house, in our offices, factory and distribution centre, works of art, photographs and sculptures by contemporary artists whom we believe have real talent and which we like. Philippe is particularly interested in photography –and also collects for himself and for our headquarters.

Hence a unique, quintessentially baroque style that we could imagine flourished in the Polish houses where we come from, a warm, personal style that is ours and is also Sisley's.

"*Art is an essential part of our life; we love being surrounded by beauty. Isabelle loves to say, 'When it is beautiful, everything goes together.'*"

On our golf course with my labrador Ophélie, a present from Valéry Giscard d'Estaing.

Our growing children; top right, golfing life with Elisabeth, Marc, Emilio and the great Spanish golf champion Seve Ballesteros.

Chapter 7

La Renaudière

La Renaudière, a place where Isabelle and I love to live, to welcome our family and friends.

“I have often said that I’ve worked to make a living, to raise my family, but also to live the life I wanted, have a place in the country to be with my family and friends.”

I have often said that I've worked to make a living, to raise my family, but also to live the life I wanted, have a place in the country to be with my family and friends, to shoot, to hunt, to breed horses that I can ride or whisper to in the evenings... to be surrounded by nature, to feel free.

Fate has been kind to me, I have been able to realize this dream: La Renaudière is located near the Loire valley in the centre of France, in the old county of Berry. Its meadows, forests, rivers and lakes had already inspired George Sand in her famous novel *La Mare au diable*. This part of France, far from the big cities and the modern world, although still aware of it, is for me one of the most beautiful places in the world. Silent, aloof, although never melancholic, the landscape that surrounds La Renaudière reminds me of the region of Malopolska in Poland, where I was born and grew up. La Renaudière and Berry are for Isabelle and me a constant source of inspiration. You can't understand Sisley without knowing and loving La Renaudière. Our home and our products reflect who we are; our soul, they bear our mark.

From La Pointerie to La Renaudière

It is only recently that the d'Ornano family arrived in the region of Berry, south of the Loire Valley. Born in Tours, my father initially rented Jarzay, a house on the outskirts of the village of Moulins-sur-Céphons. In the late 1930s he bought La Pointerie, a property off the main road near the town of Châteauroux. It includes a 19th century manor with several additions in the 20th century by the Parisian architect Alfred Trolliet. With its two wings, its square tower and flat-tiled roof, it is a handsome house. But in time it became too close to the town of Châteauroux.

I go shooting and hunting very often in the beautiful forest owned by Henry Viguier and his wife Renée in Bouges-le-Château, not far from

Henri and Renée Viguier in front of the Château de Bouges in 1963; with some friends, my father and me.

Moulins-sur-Céphons. The land is part of an estate that dates back to the High Middle Ages, on which a very beautiful 18th century château now stands. It first belonged to the La Tour d'Auvergne family, and later to the Medicis. In 1518, Madeleine de la Tour d'Auvergne (1498-1519) married Ambroise Laurent II de Medici (1492-1519), Duke of Urbino –to whom Machiavelli dedicated his famous treatise *The Prince*. They had a daughter, Catherine de Medici, the future queen of France. In 1765, on the remains of the feudal château Charles François Leblanc de Marnaval, an ironmaster and director of the Royal-warrant linen manufacturing works in Chateauroux, built the beautiful palace that stands there today; an unexpected miracle of elegance rising in the peaceful Berry countryside, with its long driveway of trees and an original English landscaped park.

With its Greek-inspired architecture and the surrounding French garden by Le Notre, the Château de Bouges is a miracle of balance and harmony, reminiscent of the "Petit Trianon" in Versailles, built at about the same time by Gabriel for the Marquise de Pompadour and which Louis XVI would later offer to his queen Marie Antoinette. In 1818, Talleyrand [1], who owned the vast Château de Valençay and its estates, acquired the Château de Bouges for his niece, Dorothée de Courlande, Duchess of Dino (1793-1862). Dorothée was probably his last love and stayed faithfully by his side in the last twenty years of his life. My wife is her great-granddaughter and she remembers her grandmother telling stories of her playing at the Château de Rochecotte, nearby, on the knees of the Duchess of Dino.

Isabelle is the great grand-daughter of Dorothée de Courlande, Duchess of Dino, Talleyrand's niece and last love, who had exceptional beauty and personality (painting by Pierre-Paul Prud'hon).

A fiery, fascinating, breathtakingly beautiful and remarkably intelligent woman, the Duchess of Dino was not easy to live with –her family and personal motto was "Rien que Dieu", an untranslatable epithet closest perhaps to "I answer only to God"– in contrast to her mother, the Duchess Anne-Dorothée de Courlande. Whatever she did or did not do, she and her sisters Wilhelmine and Pauline played an important role at the Congress of Vienna in 1815 which redrew Europe, to the extent that the three of them, along with their mother Anne-Dorothée, were called "The ladies of Courlande".

Dorothée de Courlande stayed at the Château de Bouges many times but never really settled down. She preferred the Château de Rochecotte where Talleyrand had taken up residence and where he entertained with her "everyone who was anyone at the time". He wrote in the guestbook: "Rochecotte is an enchanting place alive with questions and always just the right person to answer them."

The Duchess of Dino passed away far from France and the Berry, on her Sagan estate in Silesia, today Żagań, in Western Poland. It was probably upon reading a book about her life that Françoise Sagan got the idea of adopting this name as a pseudonym.

Since 1917, the Château de Bouges had belonged to Henri Viguier, born in 1877, owner of the famous Paris department store Bazar de l'Hôtel de Ville which he developed and modernized. In 1906 he married Renée Normant whose family from Romorantin owned the Manufacture Normant Frères, the well-known supplier of the blue cloth used for army uniforms. The Viguiers restored, redecorated and modernized the Château, which had been totally emptied of its furnishings when they bought it. Renée Viguier, with her much-respected taste, redid the interior decoration with the help of the famous Madame Doucet, a very well-known decorator then. She created a superb walled flower and vegetable garden. When not in Paris, the Viguiers gave new life to the Château and no doubt contributed to the finest chapters of its history. Elected and re-elected Mayor of Bouges from 1919 until his death, a keen horseman, Henry Viguier also had a beautiful shoot on his 3,000-hectare property. Through local politics my father and Henri Viguier became very close friends.

I will never forget the day I asked Henri Viguier to lease me the shoot at Bouges.

The Viguiers had no children and considered me a bit like their own son from the day I visited the Château de Bouges with my father –I was nine or ten at the time and fell into a manure pit! "Well done young man, that's a sign of good luck!" said the stable master. I was given a thorough bath by Madame Viguier herself and from that day became part of the family. I even ended up with my own room at the Château, today called the parrot room because of the design of its wall paper. From then on Monsieur and Madame Viguier became for me Uncle Henri and Aunt Renée.

Many years later, in 1955, Monsieur Viguier asked me to visit him at the Bazar de l'Hôtel de Ville. We talked about shooting, which he said he wanted to give up, because of his age.
"Uncle Henri, why don't you lease me your shoot?"
"Why not?"

The shoot at Bouges in the 1950s. Top middle photograph, with Henri Viguier; below: Renée Viguier.

Sometime later he brought it up again:
"Actually, I won't lease it, I'm giving it to you. On condition you maintain and preserve it, and continue to invite my friends."

I was really overwhelmed, blown away by his gesture and by what it meant. It was well known that the shoot at Bouges was one of the most beautiful in France. I knew every inch of the forest, as I have so often hunted and ridden on horseback in it with Isabelle. I know its small and large game, deer, roe deer, wild boar, pheasant and duck –its trees and flora hold no secrets for me. I would now be in charge of it, responsible for it!

For some 15 years, I have organized pheasant shoots in Bouges. We have invited many guests, including some of the best shots from all around the world. At the edge of the forest, La Renaudière was an 18th century shooting lodge on the property, restored by Madame Viguier. Shooting lunches and dinners in the early years were held at the Château de Bouges. Madame Viguier passed away in May 1966 and her husband soon after in August 1967. I didn't want to take over the Bouges château, as Prime Minister Georges Pompidou suggested, as I felt it did not belong to the family. Henri Viguier had left the Château and a couple of farms to what is now the Centre des Monuments Nationaux. The upkeep and the organization of visits are paid for by the estate's income. Between La Renaudière and La Pointerie, twenty-five kilometres away we continued the Viguiers' hunting and shooting tradition, before selling the latter in 1973 and making La Renaudière our country home.

We took on La Renaudière not simply to own the place, but to preserve it and embellish it. We added to the forest four farms and various buildings, including the farmhouse called La Renaudière, which was behind the shooting lodge. The two buildings were combined, creating a courtyard. La Renaudière is a warm, comfortable farmhouse, beautifully arranged by Isabelle with the help of the great Danish landscape architect and close friend Mogens Twede who had been married to her great aunt, Princess Dolly Radziwill.

It is here that we come to rest and recuperate. As far back as I can remember I've spent every month of August, without exception, at La Renaudière. I'm not too keen on the sea and the mountains and unlike my brother Michel, and I'm not a city person. My Polish blood makes me at heart a country man, happy to be surrounded by nature with my dogs and my horses, always busy with the thousand-and-one daily chores that a big property entails, with all the people who work on it.

The children spent all their childhood vacations here. The boys helped on the farm during the holidays, gathering the hay and the harvest and being paid five francs an hour. They played with the children from the neighbouring village. In those days they used to organize village football tournaments that brought dozens of teams of all ages together. Sadly those times have gone with the young people leaving for the cities.

I love animals, and they have always accompanied us. Dogs of course, but also a wild boar called Suzie. Her mother was killed by mistake and we rescued her as a baby. Three years later, Suzie had become an intelligent and malicious young lady weighing 100 kilos. She used to open the door of her kennel with her nose, sneak up silently and knock over the table on which afternoon tea was set. She always managed to eat the sandwiches and fruit before being caught! Unfortunately, we eventually had to release her back into the wild – into her own world.

Another amusing adoption was Kiki, a baby sparrow I had found fallen from its nest and which I fed and brought back to Paris. It used to sleep in my bathtub and didn't like it at all when I took a bath! Unable to fly in the long corridor of our apartment, Kiki used to hop down it on foot. The children, of course, loved it. We finally had to release it, because it soiled the curtains and lampshades, to Isabelle's great annoyance. We set it free under the same oak tree from which it had fallen. Our sparrow returned three times, before flying away for ever.

Anne Potocka, Isabelle's sister, really loved La Renaudière.

It is at La Renaudière that we like to entertain our friends and family. Isabelle's older sister Anne often came and loved riding. She spent a lot of time with us here but unfortunately she passed away prematurely. We remodelled the two farms surrounding the shooting lodge. We created the Garden of the Madonna, the Orchard, a kitchen garden and stables. The house is surrounded by beautiful trees and we have also planted new species. These have now become big trees. Isabelle placed sculptures in the garden. Little by little I drew up the plans and built a 4-hole golf course, with a combination of 18 tees and a lake which is a water obstacle much feared by our guests! We both love to play it.

The golf course around the lake in La Renaudière.

We also built a tennis court with roses climbing around, and a swimming pool where we spend a lot of time in the summer and where we have had memorable parties, the last being one this year, for our 50th wedding anniversary, with an orchestra which the children had arranged to come from Ukraine. On that occasion, we also had a Mass celebrated under the biggest oak tree in the garden which was attended by the whole family, friends of the children as well as many locals.

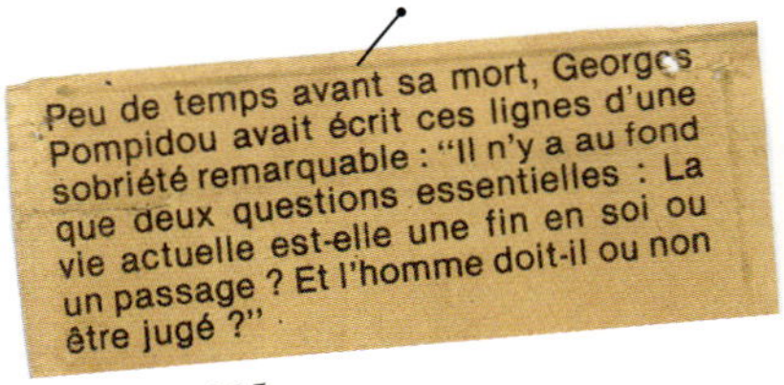
Peu de temps avant sa mort, Georges Pompidou avait écrit ces lignes d'une sobriété remarquable : "Il n'y a au fond que deux questions essentielles : La vie actuelle est-elle une fin en soi ou un passage ? Et l'homme doit-il ou non être jugé ?"

(*) *cf.* p.135.

I must not forget, in these pages about Bouges and La Renaudière, to mention the people who between our Paris and Berry homes worked for us and accompanied us in our daily life. They watched our children grow, our friends come and go and some of our dear ones pass away, always providing a warm and friendly service for all of us. The heart and soul of La Renaudière was Gérard Gausset, who recently passed away. He worked for us for nearly 40 years and his cooking and bouquets were legendary. They all mingled discreetly with the celebrities, politicians, ambassadors, artists, academics, journalists who were our frequent guests. They ensured that our numerous shoots, hunts, receptions and weddings were perfectly organized.

Isabelle with Georges Pompidou, Prime Minister from 1962 to 1969, then President of France from 1969 to 1974...

Two holidays marked these privileged moments, Christmas and Easter. It used to take at least two days to set up the big traditional Christmas tree, arrange the nativity scene, decorate the chimney, etc. Every year we were all so happy to see the house thus decorated. Then came Easter, which was always a time of great excitement. Easter was the opportunity to make traditional Polish cakes, the *Sernik* cheesecake and the *Mazurki*, big rectangular cakes garnished with marzipan, oranges, prunes or even chocolate. The word Alleluia was written on the top and a sprig of blessed boxwood put in the middle. There was a lot of hustle and bustle in the kitchen and all around the house.

As I have already said, we had many guests come to shoot. I'd like to mention three or four, begging the others will excuse me as I cannot mention them all. Georges Pompidou, who honoured us both with his friendship as Prime Minister, and as President of France. Georges Pompidou was a round man, both literally and figuratively, of exceptional intelligence, driven by the desire to be true to himself and to achieve, without giving material things the importance they didn't deserve. Authority and power never prevented him from being natural, always himself, meeting people on their terms and listening to everyone. One day, when we were driving between the Pointerie and La Renaudière he asked us to stop the car in the village of Levroux:

"Let us stop in this cafe, I would like to smoke a cigarette with the locals and have a drink."

He went in and immediately began talking to the customers...

It was typical of President Pompidou. We both had great respect for him.

... and with Marie-Claire Pauwels and Valéry Giscard d'Estaing, longtime Minister of Economy and Finance, President of France from 1974 to 1981, two close friends.

He was not indifferent to spiritual matters either. We always recall the words he wrote shortly before he died:

"There are ultimately only two basic questions: Is life an end in itself or a journey to something else? And will or will not men be judged for it?"(*)

Georges Pompidou died in office. We remained close to his wife Claude, as well as Edouard Balladur, Georges Pompidou's Secretary-General of the Elysée when he was President, who subsequently became Prime Minister.

The sudden death of Georges Pompidou in 1974 allowed Valéry Giscard d'Estaing to become President of France. After seven positive years of presidency, his defeat in the 1981 Presidential elections prevented him from fulfilling his political potential, a bit like my brother whose death greatly affected him. We have remained close friends.

Among our guests during the 1960s were the Duke and Duchess of Windsor. We often went to their home in the Bois de Boulogne and their country house The Moulin de la Tuilerie at Gif-sur-Yvette, south of Paris. A surprising destiny for he who had been King Edward VIII for less than a year. Events had run their course a quarter of a century earlier when, on 11 December 1936, the King of England chose to abdicate because he could not be King without, in his own words, "the help and support of the woman I love".

Despite their popularity, elegance and style they were now the victims of the life imposed on them by the King's abdication in 1936. Hence the Duke's determination for his wife to be recognized as his equal even though the British royal family continued to refuse the Duchess of Windsor the title of Her Royal Highness. And hence the long twilight of a shared, rather uninteresting life, marked by what seemed to us an indescribable melancholy in someone who had been Prince of Wales and for a short time King of the immense British Empire. I think that what they liked in La Renaudière was an atmosphere somewhat similar to that of the country houses in England where they could no longer live.

Many of our friends have come here again and again. This place offers a breath of fresh air; ideal for shooting, hunting, riding or other sports, in cold or hot weather, come rain or shine as the Berry has its own distinctive climate.

And how can I not mention golf! A difficult but such an amusing sport, which has given us much pleasure. We both love playing golf,

Golf, a passion which Isabelle and I share.

and the fact that both of us play more or less well has given us a lot of pleasure, particularly in the United States during our business trips. We have been invited to play on superb golf courses such as Cypress Point, on the Monterrey Peninsula in California, surrounded by the Pacific Ocean. But probably what we enjoyed most was, and still is, the Windsor Golf Club and "Village on the sea" near Vero Beach in Florida. Created on what was a grapefruit grove, by Galen and Hilary Weston, the golf course is beautiful, the endless beach and the whole village a corner of paradise. The Westons, who own department stores with which we work in both Canada and England, have become dear friends.

With Isabelle, we have often played and won competitions together. But our claim to fame remains the Mortefontaine Club Championship. We won it in 1973, I the men's and Isabelle the Ladies' category even though she was nine months' pregnant! Christine was born five days later! Of all our children, the most gifted and passionate golfer was our second son Marc. Unfortunately God cut short his ambitions.

Hunting, a state of mind

Ever since my childhood in Poland, nature, hunting and shooting have been among my life's passions. I've had the opportunity to enjoy exceptional shooting and hunting in France and abroad, in terms of scenery and organization. I have organized partridge and pheasant shoots at Bouges and have also been to beautiful shoots in England and in Spain, and have hunted in Austria. In the shoots in Bouges, we would have 30 to 40 beaters, 7 gamekeepers and a dozen guns, each with a loader who kept two guns alternately loaded. At the end of the day the game was laid out and all the participants, beaters, game keepers and loaders were thanked. In France, hunting and shooting are very deeply rooted in country life traditions and everyone is passionate about it, respectful of the animals and of the need for conservation.

Hunting and shooting have their rules, ethics, and of course their dress code –which have to be respected. In the mid-1970s we stopped the pheasant shoots that required lots of beaters, employees and gamekeepers. They had become too costly at the time when all our efforts were focused on Sisley.

The hunt, a state of mind when one loves nature and animals.

In hunting what I really like is the planning beforehand, the stalking, the long walks, the tactics and observation. I can look at a beautiful stag or roe dear for hours and not shoot. I love the anticipation, starting before dawn, accompanied by a keeper, walking for hours in the forest, creeping up, silently observing the animals and perhaps picking out one to be shot. Hunting is synonymous with respect, not with destruction; it is a challenge for the eye. Shooting is more of a sport, and of course a matter of territory and of organization.

I feel responsible for the forest and for the animals that live in it. I want to preserve it by caring for its fauna and flora, and the astonishing life within it. The increase in the number of stag and wild boar has reduced the number of roe dear, and as we have created lakes within the forest there are more duck and fewer pheasants, which we used to breed. I have enclosed the whole butterfly shaped 3,000-acre Bouges forest, to prevent the wild animals from damaging the neighbouring farmland, and have continuously repaired and maintained the paths and alleys and preserved the beautiful oak trees along them. I learnt this from Monsieur and Madame Viguier. Madame Viguier did not like to see trees cut. Most of the felling was therefore done deeper in the woods, where no one could see! We should never forget the example of those who have preceded us.

I'm happy that my son Philippe loves shooting and hunting and is a first class shot. His approach to nature is somewhat different to mine, and he has described it in a lovely book, Les Trajectoires Inverses, which he dedicated to me. I love the final words: "The wind changes, night is falling. The boars come out, their fearless young are frolic-king. The forest changes but never ages." And above all: hunting is "another world".

A man's best friend

I cannot talk of hunting without mentioning my dogs who were constantly at my side. I will never forget my four-legged friends. Two of them in particular, spent all their lives (always too short) with us, accompanied me everywhere, in the city, to the office and in the country: Ophélie, a Labrador that Valéry Giscard d'Estaing gave me (he loved this breed perfect for picking up birds) and Frac who was a present from Paloma Botin, my daughter Elisabeth's mother in law, and had a unique personality. Anticipating all my wishes, they could do everything but speak. I was lucky to have got them as puppies. Dogs become the image of their masters; they reflect how they have been brought up.

Horses, a passion

I am, as were my father and my brother, a horse lover, but in my case especially trotters. When after the war we began making money with our first business, I was able to buy and breed horses. My father had a very good stud farm at Manneville, which included one or two broodmare trotters. Of course, thoroughbreds are the noblest, but trotters are much easier to breed and trotting races, because of the betting, have become extremely popular in France. Keen to boost the image of trotting races –which are mainly practiced in France, Germany, Italy, Scandinavia and the United States– René Ballière who was the great man of the post-war trotting races in France and who happened to be a good friend of mine, persuaded us to create Le Cercle des Amateurs de Trot, meaning a Club of Trotting Amateurs. With my brother Michel and his friends, we "gentlemen drivers" ran amateur races in France, across the Rhine, in Italy and in Switzerland. Open to the public, registered in France with the PMU racecourse operators association, they were always exciting events with a huge following. I won about 20 races and as many Cups which are now lined up in my library.

With Frac, who was my companion for many years.

In 1952, René Ballière also came up with the idea of holding night time races on a floodlit track in Vincennes, which became a very important race course, the biggest race track in the Paris area, exclusively for trotters, with several restaurants, and able to hold a large number of spectators. He also changed the name of the Société du Demi-Sang to Société d'Encouragement à l'Élevage du Cheval Français, only for trotters. This decision, which did not seem that important at the time, would stimulate the recognition of French trotters as a breed in its own right. My father, Michel and I were active members of both the Société d'Encouragement à l'Élevage du Cheval Français (French Thoroughbred Commission) and the Comité du Trot Français (French trotting commission).

In 1962, Ballière, with our support, founded the Grosbois training centre, just 30 minutes from the Hippodrome of Paris-Vincennes.

It is a beautiful place with all the most modern facilities, training tracks, some of them under cover for the winter season, and of course the best specialists, vets and equipment.

We discontinued these amateur races when Michel became Mayor of Deauville, and later a Member of Parliament. No doubt, racing and politics don't mix well in France! Absorbed by Orlane and later on by Sisley I left racing behind. My father Guillaume d'Ornano kept up the family torch with thoroughbreds such as Misti. In 1982 he stopped breeding, and sold the Haras de Manneville. I then recovered the two broodmare trotters that were there, Ekiane and Nekiane, and bought two other mares and thus started my own breeding stud farm at La Renaudière.

Although breeding trotters has been in constant progress, breeding them outside Normandy, the French breeding region, and more so developing a racing stable and winning the big classics, is no easy achievement. Not all foals, with or without first class pedigrees, whether bred at home or bought as yearlings, become champions! Very few actually make it: many disappoint, some unfortunately get

I win an amateur trotting race.

RTL
FRA DIAVOLO - 22.12.96
Y. DREUX
PRIX DE VINCENNES - 2700M
GROUPE I

FRA DIAVOLO

injured in training or competition, and few will go on to make excellent breeders. Making it to the winners' enclosure of a classic race therefore signifies real excellence. It's not a lottery, at least I've never believed so and never used those words –it takes constant effort, attention and obstinacy. As I always do, when I took up breeding trotters, I tried to do it as well as possible, and was very demanding with the people around me.

The family d'Ornano, the jockey Yves Dreux and the trainer Ali Hawas in December 1996. Fra Diavolo had just won the Prix de Vincennes.

I was helped by two great professionals, Ali Hawas, one of the best French trainers, and later by Fabrice Souloy, one of the rising stars of the new generation. On the farm itself I was helped by Claude Liégeois, assisted by Philippe Coutant, who has been with us since his teens and who has a true passion for horses and breeding. Thanks to everyone, I've been rewarded with superb horses and some great victories. Luck perhaps, but also the result of persevering, as usual…

In February 2010, another exceptional horse, Private Love, trained by Fabrice Souloy and ridden by Mathieu Abrivard, wins the Prix de Paris, the great trotting classic in France.

In 1987, an excellent trotter, Villebon –the name of one of my farms– was born at La Renaudière. With a good pedigree, well bred, well raised, well trained, he won seven or eight races, two of which being semi-classics. The following year, six foals were born; four of them went on to win races at Vincennes. Five years later came Fra Diavolo and at the age of three, on December 23rd 1996, this very beautiful trotter perfectly ridden by the brilliant jockey Yves Dreux won one of the three great French classics, the prestigious Prix de Vincennes. Fra Diavolo was unfortunately injured some time later –maybe even during the race– and his career was finished. We sold him and he became a stallion for several years. In 1997 I bought an excellent horse, Ivan d'Ocagnes, who won many races. However, two years later I decided to stop breeding racehorses at La Renaudière –again it had become very expensive when we were developing Sisley.

But the passion never faded. In 2006, I bought a few race horses to start all over again. Jean-Pierre Dubois the well-known French breeder of trotters gave me the choice between a male and a filly –I hesitated but happily my trainer, Fabrice Souloy, persuaded me to buy the filly, Private Love. This exceptional mare who showed signs of great potential (though not always consistent), went on to win ten races, including the great trotting classic. That day, Sunday February 21st 2010, with a four-pound handicap, the beautiful Private Love was not the favourite. Perfectly ridden by Mathieu Abrivard under the instructions of my trainer Fabrice Souloy, she won easily, after a remarkable race, Le Grand Prix de Paris.

Two great prizes, Vincennes and Paris, dozens of other races –my equestrian adventure ended well! Victories are sweet when they have been well prepared.

Chapter 8

Sisley, a French and international family business

Philippe and I in 2003.

"At the beginning of the twenty first century, Sisley is present in over 90 countries on each continent and has continued to grow whilst remaining true to its values."

At the beginning of the twenty-first century, Sisley is present in over 90 countries on each continent and has continued to grow while remaining true to its values and firmly cultivating its unique core beliefs: creativity, perfectionism and passion for its products –values shared by all our employees.

A family business…

We have remained an independent family business including, of course, those of our children who wished to join Sisley.

Our children grew up with Sisley, surrounded by perfumes and beauty products that Isabelle and I would try out daily. Those who chose to work with us experienced both the good and bad times and have always been aware of the work which we put into developing the company. We never really talked about anything but Sisley, they recall with humour! From the age of 15, some of them started to earn pocket money putting promotional cards into envelopes, sticking on stamps, and carefully writing names and addresses on them by hand. They would work at the switchboard before going on to do summer jobs in department stores selling our products. I'm pleased to see several of my grandchildren following the same path as trainees in the business. Whatever their occupation in the future will be, it is wonderful to see them adopting work values early in life.

We have five children: Philippe (1964), Marc (1966), Elisabeth (1968), Laetitia (1970) and Christine (1973). Philippe now runs Sisley, assisted by Christine and Elisabeth. Only Laetitia did not want to join the family business. We did not create Sisley with the aim of passing it on to our children. The notion of a family business is only possible if they are capable and willing. Otherwise, in today's open world economy, they would inevitably find themselves put aside, in this very competitive field. These days you don't risk a precious and solid legacy on someone who is not up to the job, just because they are part of your family. Those who are capable and are surrounded by a good team will continue what can be an extraordinary human adventure, while the others are forced to sell. When Sisley increased in size, we were approached by numerous candidates. When we realized that our children were interested in the business and capable of succeeding, Isabelle and I decided that Sisley would be a family business, a family brand.

It all began for us with a terrible tragedy, an immense grief. Marc, our second son, joined the business very early. He wanted to make a career out of it. Although only 20, Marc was a born salesman with innate business acumen, as well as being sensitive; he was a man of action. On September 24th 1986 driving to Orléans, his car was hit by a lorry. Marc was twenty. As he had wished, he is buried in the d'Ornano tomb at Bouges-le-Chateau, where Anne, Isabelle's sister also lies. In his memory, and to preserve his legacy, in 1990 we created the Sisley-Marc d'Ornano Scholarship at INSEAD, the Fontainebleau Business School. It was at that same time that Poland became a democracy again. This scholarship is offered to a young Polish graduate, so as to allow him or her to contribute to the economic development of their country.

Marc d'Ornano (1966-1986).

After studying Law and Economics, Philippe was preparing to leave for Atlanta in the United States where the New York Times Group had offered him a job. But with Marc gone, he offered to stay with us and join Sisley instead. Starting, as was the family tradition, as a sales rep, initially in France –Paris, the North, the Southwest, the Cote d'Azur– "swallowing up" kilometres every week. In late 1988,

Philippe became Sales Manager for France. As for me, I focused on our international business, which was taking off. He took charge of the European markets in 1991, and worked alongside us, before becoming Managing Director in 1999, and then Deputy CEO in 2006. In 2013, he became Chairman of Sisley's Executive Board. I became chairman of the Supervisory Board, with Isabelle as Vice Chair.

Philippe and his wife Mina.

In addition to loving nature, as I do, Philippe is an avid sportsman, an expert surfer and a fan of rugby. He is also a great lover of books, and writes poetry in his spare time. Like me, he is very attached to his family. In 1993 he married Mina Panicevic and they have three children Milena, Shaya and Eliya.

With a great operational and visual capacity, as well as having my acute sense of detail, Philippe helped us to successfully accomplish Sisley's evolution. We worked together very closely, but also with great professionalism, essential in a family business in which most of the managers are not members of the family.

Elisabeth helped us enormously throughout the Nineties, being the face of the brand worldwide. She told me that one of her first olfactory memories was Eau de Campagne, which I liked to perfume my handkerchiefs with! In 1989, Elisabeth married Emilio Botín-Sanz de Sautuola. They live in Madrid and have four children: Daria, Emilio, Huberto and Luis. She is a member of our Executive Board. In Madrid, she runs the Elisabeth d'Ornano Association for hyperactive children. The aim of the association is to educate and inform parents, teachers and paediatricians on the best way to raise these children whose behaviour is sometimes difficult and upsetting. Emilio, very busy with his own business affairs, agreed to become a member of the Board of the Sisley Foundation.

As for Christine, she joined Sisley after starting her career in the United States. She studied comparative literature at Princeton University in the US, before beginning her professional career in New York as a buyer at Saks Fifth Avenue –an experience that would prove invaluable when we persuaded her to join Sisley in 1997. Like her sisters, Christine had lived in Spain and spoke fluent Spanish. She was only 24 when I asked her to create our subsidiary in Mexico. "You speak Spanish, you are perfect for the job."

Christine succeeded brilliantly in developing our brand there, a market similar to the United States in terms of cosmetics culture. She set up our subsidiary with the help of Sisley's then CEO Alain Denoly, created a strong business relationship with the luxury department store chain Palacio de Hierro and built a top-quality team. Nearly two decades later she is happy to see that most of the team is still there. She went on to develop the brand in Brazil, Argentina, Colombia, Venezuela, Uruguay and Paraguay. Thanks to her, the brand has grown strongly in South America, creating trusted relationships with our distributors. We have now opened in Peru and Chile as well and have established our own subsidiary in Brazil.

Having worked his way up in the company, Philippe became Chairman of Sisley's Executive Board in 2013.

At one point, as often happens, Argentina was hit heavily by the economic crisis. Mrs Castrogiovanni, our manager there, came to see me in tears expecting us to shut down our operations. I told her, "Become my distributor, keep the stock to help you get started. Business

Christine is today Senior Vice President and on the Executive Board of Sisley.

is bad right now but it will improve."

Mrs Castrogiovanni kept crying, but no longer for the same reason! Over the years, with her husband, she made Sisley one of the leaders in luxury cosmetics in her country.

At my request, Christine returned to Europe and in 1999, she took over the development of our Sisley subsidiary in the UK and Ireland, based in London. It was an important mission, more difficult than it appeared, even though Sisley had a strong position in some prestigious stores such as Harrods and Harvey Nichols. The UK, for a luxury brand like ours, is a market of department stores and we only wanted our products to be sold in the best. Christine built up Sisley in England and Scotland with finesse and patience. She hired qualified people, carefully developed its retail distribution by opening for Sisley counters in stores such as Selfridges, as well as other major department stores. In the U.K. Sisley has an excellent image and the clients who enjoy our products appreciate their quality and the fact that they are plant based, offering everything that is expected from a superb line of cosmetics.

Now Senior Vice President and on the company's Executive Board, Christine has a very good business sense. She is creative, with a good eye for anything to do with the visual side of Sisley. She works with Isabelle, Philippe and their in-house teams on all creative aspects of the brand, as well as the new products. In 2003, Christine married

With Elisabeth during her wedding to Emilio Botín-Sanz de Sautuola.

Marzouk Al Bader, but unfortunately they are now divorced. She has three children: Alma, Isabelle and Inès.

Laetitia is the only one of our children who was not interested in Sisley. A brilliant and original journalist, she was a reporter for eight years for *Madame Figaro*, a magazine that sent her all around the world. She left her job to do a Master in Human Ecology in Edinburgh. Her end-of-program thesis on Black Madonnas is often quoted [(1)]. Laetitia pursued her own career in ecology and sustainable development. Unfortunately, after being ill for some years, Laetitia passed away on November 29th 2013. This has been another immense sorrow for us.

Being a family business also means making sure we maintain and preserve the Sisley corporate culture. My management philosophy, which Philippe shares, is based on availability, trust, loyalty, and expectation. One of my greatest satisfactions is the fact that, throughout its growth and the steady recruitment of 4,000 employees both in France and abroad, Sisley has kept its unique core values – the basis of its collective internal strength.

We want to stay independent. Philippe – as Co-President along with another dynamic and committed businesswoman, Elisabeth Ducottet –now also runs the ASMEP-ETI, the Association of Medium-Size and Family Companies which brings together many businesses like ours. It was founded by Yvon Gattaz who was the former "President du Patronat Français". I have a lot of admiration and friendship for him. His tireless work enabled the unblocking of the transmission of medium size businesses in France. Our country owes him a lot, and Philippe, along with others, has been heavily involved at his side.

1. "Has the archetype of the Black Madonna a role to play in reconciling spirit and matter and healing the split between humans and nature?". Master in Human Ecology, 2003, quoted by «Les religions traditionnelles et la foi en Jésus-Christ [Traditional religions and Jesus-Christ's faith]», *Bulletin CPCM* [Christians to Change The World], November 27th, 20, 2004.

In France...

All Sisley products are formulated, developed and produced in France. Our growth has in no way changed the plant-based approach to beauty that has been ours since the beginning. The improving processes and techniques have helped our business growth and that has in turn given our R&D more resources to develop the phytotherapy research which we have helped pioneer.

In 2003, we bought a factory in Blois, on the banks of the Loire. It was transformed, modernized and expanded, and we now produce all our skin care products there. During the six years, I was personally involved in this operation along with Philippe and Philippe Valentin. We tripled the site's surface area from 7,000 to 23,000 m^2 and quadrupled its production capacity to be able to match the pace of our constantly increasing sales. One of the most modern tools of its generation, designed to meet the highest standards in terms of quality control and environmental requirements, it allows the production of all the cosmetics that we sell in France and throughout the world. Isabelle, with her impeccable sense of taste and detail, oversaw the decor of the entire site and chose with me the 1,600 trees that have been planted around the buildings. Whenever we go there we are happy to see them grow.

When we first bought this factory in Blois it was in great difficulty. True to our tradition, one month after the takeover, we organized our Christmas lunch, just as we do at all our other sites. A woman approached me and said kindly: "When we knew Sisley was buying our company, we thought: "We've hit the jackpot!" She was right to trust us. Ten years on, we have multiplied the number of employees by five.

Our distribution centre in Gennevilliers, which housed our global logistics, research centre, and part of our administrative services, was much too small for our growth. Not only was this the price of success, but it had become a real problem. It was not easy to find a site within

Sisleÿa Global Anti-âge, one of Sisley's bestsellers.

the Paris area with good transportation links to meet our needs. We had more than 250 employees working there, some of them for many years and we did not want to lose them.

However, in 2009 we succeeded. We bought land and, after obtaining the necessary permits and carrying out the building, in January 2011 we began operations at our new centre in Saint-Ouen-L'Aumône, north-west of Paris. What once was a field became an ultra-modern site within two years. This was overseen by Philippe, along with his team, Philippe Valentin, Philippe Lacassagne and André Reich. It enabled us to combine all the activities that had previously been spread throughout several buildings in Gennevilliers. We have thus multiplied by four our logistics and greatly expanded our laboratories. Once again Isabelle helped us with all the interior decor and the surroundings.

Since the completion of our new facilities, we have continued to recruit. In ten years we have invested nearly €150 million in our company. The Blois and Saint-Ouen-L'Aumône sites have provided total satisfaction and the number of staff has almost doubled. These projects, successfully undertaken by our teams, are proof of Sisley's ambition and will allow us to continue with our development.

My firm belief has always been that the success of a brand has to be built patiently and based on exceptional products.

Cosmetics, according to Sisley, are the result of an enduring effort. What makes a cream effective is not just an amazing exotic extract discovered somewhere in the Amazon that can be highlighted in its advertising! The secret of a good product is understanding how the skin works, and a complete scientific solution for each cosmetic need. We like the term "global" used in the names of many of our creations; it defines this philosophy well; create a complete product. This term, which we were the first to use, has now been much copied.

The Francos factory near Blois enables us to respond to Sisley's ongoing development.

One of the courtyards at the logistics and research center in Saint-Ouen-l'Aumône, with the sculpture "I am you" by Nicolas Alquin.

Two of the company's stands. Working with Sisley, a state of mind.

It took ten years to create our star product –Sisleÿa Global Anti Age– an unrivalled face cream containing 50 different active ingredients. Intensive research is required to develop the precise concentrations and combination of the many ingredients which will result in the final product we desire. Texture is also essential as it plays a key role in providing the pleasure in the application of a cosmetic. This is something appreciated by Sisley's consumers worldwide and a belief firmly held by Elisabeth and Christine, who test every product.

Because the product itself is central to Sisley, we offer trial samples and we rely on expert, trained beauticians who are able to explain, demonstrate and recommend each of our products. Their reports are carefully studied and Sisley continues to sell the cult products that have made its reputation. For a clientele to believe in Sisley and keep returning, professional advice is essential and we know what we owe to our teams in this field. Selling is a real talent and a worthy occupation, not always easy, and unfortunately in France it is not always regarded and respected as much as it deserves.

In the 2000s, we introduced Sisleÿa, in 2002, the foundation Phyto-Teint Eclat, a smooth, extremely fluid formula that is one of France's best-selling high-end make up foundations. In 2005, we launched All Day All Year, an anti-age formula with UVA filters in a unique encapsulation process to protect the skin from all external environmental damage. In 2005 too, we offered Hydra Global, a highly intensive moisturizing fluid cream. In 2009, we introduced another great product, Supremÿa, a night time anti-age formula which pushes back the skin's genetically programmed aging process, compensates for damage suffered by the skin during the day and prepares it for the next day.

In 2006, sixteen years after the launch of Eau du Soir, we launched a third perfume, Soir de Lune, the result of many years of work with Isabelle. A lovely, romantic, chypre fragrance with an evocative name –a night of love declared. Soir de Lune is a subtle, unique, sophisticated and very feminine fragrance, a combination of roses, jasmine

Our apartment in London,
a source of inspiration
for the perfume Soir de Lune.

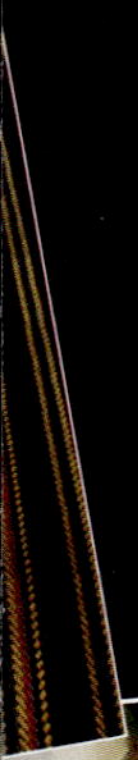

and mimosa. Its first advertising campaign was inspired by the eclectic and original atmosphere created by Isabelle in our London Knightsbridge house which we have had since the early 1980s. As with Eau du Soir, Bronislaw Krzysztof designed a sculpted cap, a moon with a feminine face. Three years later, came the three Eaux de Sisley –elegant, delicate and fresh– three sisters, three moods, three facets of the same woman.

Eau d'Ikar,
our first perfume for men.

Men also use our products, not only the cosmetics but the perfumes too. Although their skin is more resistant than women's, it is exposed daily to the damaging effects of shaving, stress and environmental pollution. In general, men want an all-in-one solution –a single cream to apply daily which meets all their needs. To respond to this demand, we launched Sisleyum in 2011. The same year, we introduced our first perfume for men– Eau d'Ikar. It reinterprets the myth of Icarus, that of the beauty and fragility of the modern man, a mixture of ambition, risk-taking, courage and sensuality. The composition of this perfume is unique. Its main essence, lentiscus, is extracted from that aromatic shrub found in the Corsican mountains, a reminder of our family roots. Even though I love Eau d'Ikar, I still remain loyal to "my" Eau de Campagne!

… and internationally

Since the 1990s, in the wake of the collapse of the Berlin Wall and all it represented, the political barriers separating our continent have fallen. Countries that were once isolated have now rapidly developed. New consumers have appeared in these emerging countries – which have now emerged!

Sisley has made the most of this opportunity, selling our products in new countries through distributors, followed by subsidiaries.

Our first distributor for Spain simply fell in love with the brand during a trip to Paris. We were still in our little office on the Champs-Elysées when el Sr. Montenegro came to visit us. He had just discovered Sisley at Galeries Lafayette.
"I'm Spanish, very well connected, I have a sister with a perfumery shop in the Puerta del Sol in Madrid, and I absolutely want to sell your products in Spain!".

A friend of all the major Spanish perfumers, he introduced Sisley in the 50 best perfumery shops in Spain straight away, and so the brand was launched in this country to which my wife is so attached.

The story was the same with Japan, when Mr Yang, the President of the subsidiary of a major international cosmetic company also discovered us in a French department store during a trip to Paris.
"Your cosmetic line is exceptional. I would like to distribute it in Japan where I know a lot of people. To do so, I will resign as President of my present cosmetic company."

He kept his word and devoted himself entirely to promoting Sisley. But launching a country like Japan means getting involved personally. Isabelle travelled to Japan several times, where she was shown around by Kumi Taniguchi, the beautiful wife of the famous architect Yoshio Taniguchi, well-known in public relations back then, who has remained a friend we both like very much. We returned to Tokyo for the launch party organised by Mr Yang. The Japanese, being very interested in phyto-cosmetology, appreciated Sisley's products. And because they also love history, we had the marshal's baton belonging to Philippe-Antoine d'Ornano sent over from France as well as life-size copies of his portrait and that of Marie Walewska. It was an immense success.

We grew rapidly in Asia, despite the 1996-1997 Asian financial crisis which affected a number of its young economies to varying degrees. Fortunately it was only temporary. We started out extremely well in South Korea, that very dynamic country, as we introduced our line early on, just as the country had opened up. We enjoyed an excellent relationship with a major, high-quality local distributor who dedicated one of his divisions to our brand and thus we occupied a very good position in that market from the start.

A combination of circumstances and the consequences of the Asian crisis, however, led us to create our own subsidiary in South Korea in 1998. Mr Hong, who was in charge of the distribution of our brand there, called me one day saying, "My parent company is having problems. I have to stop distributing Sisley in South Korea, lay off the staff involved, including me, and return your stock. Where should I send it?".

I thought for a few seconds before saying, "How many of you in South Korea work for Sisley?"
"80 people."
"Ok, I'll buy back the stock, I'll re-employ all your staff and you will be the manager of our future South Korean subsidiary."

At a recent dinner in Paris with the 50 managers of all our subsidiaries, in response to the general question, "What has been the most memorable moment in your professional careers?" Out of the group Mr Hong stood up: "When Hubert d'Ornano told me on the phone in the late 1990s that he would re-employ everyone and create a subsidiary in my country, of which I would be the manager!"

He has developed our company beautifully and South Korea is today one of our biggest markets.

The Sisley-d'Ornano Foundation

In 2007, we created the Sisley-d'Ornano Foundation. It is under the aegis of the Fondation de France, with 97% of donations going directly to aid our causes. Among the actions undertaken in the field of art, the Foundation has participated in the restoration of the dome and fresco of Notre-Dame de l'Assomption church, rue Saint-Honoré in the heart of the capital which in 1844 became the Polish Church of Paris. The fresco was painted in the 18th century by the French painter Charles de La Fosse, the painter of the dome frescoes of the Invalides and of the Royal Chapel at the Château de Versailles. It equally enabled all the beautiful paintings inside the church to be restored.

The Foundation also funded the new Gabriel bell, as part of the restoration of the eight bells of Notre-Dame-de-Paris Cathedral. The bell was cast and engraved by the traditional Cornille-Havard foundry, in Normandy. As a result, Notre-Dame now has all its original bells which after 220 years ring as they did before the French Revolution. The new set of bells rang out for the first time on Saturday March 23rd 2013, to mark the cathedral's 850th anniversary.

In the field of social philanthropy, the Sisley-d'Ornano Foundation has rebuilt and upgraded the Bergerie de Faucon hostel managed by l'Association du Père Gilbert, for young criminals, allowing it to reopen and accommodate young people in great difficulty. It also supports the "Nature et Aventure" association which organizes trips for disadvantaged children from Gennevilliers, the Kids Company which helps vulnerable children in London, and the Sumba Foundation's programme providing school meals and fighting malnutrition on the Indonesian island of Sumba.

In the medical field, the Foundation awards the Sisley-Jérôme-Lejeune International Prize for Genetics Research into Down's syndrome. The Foundation has also participated in a study on palliative care for terminally sick children in collaboration with the Palliative Care Foundation. It supports a beauty programme for women suffering from cancer, and funds the association set up by Elisabeth d'Ornano in Spain to provide information and education for parents and teachers of hyperactive children. It has adopted five young pupils within the foundation of the Legion of Honour. They are good students from very underprivileged backgrounds and they will be helped through university, up to their first job –the results are very promising!

It would be too long to mention each country where we work, but they are all dear to our hearts. We have visited almost all of them, hired our teams or worked with the teams of our distributors, visited the cities, met customers, the press, consumers. We have given a lot of thought as to how best develop our brand. I loved working in Italy; it is one of the most beautiful countries in the world.

Present in more than ninety countries, including Asia, Sisley is an international company and a worldwide brand.

We are proud to have created a subsidiary in Poland, Isabelle's homeland. Who could have dreamt of that in the 1980s? Every month, we welcome to our home in Paris groups of sales people who sell Sisley all around the world. We enjoy meeting them and it is the highlight of their trips to Paris!

Today, in the United Arab Emirates, South Africa, Ukraine, Brazil and the Philippines to name a few, Philippe and Christine, as well as our export teams continue this adventure.

Being a global brand, Sisley continues its dynamic growth. Our products target relatively well-off middle class working women, the number of which is constantly growing in today's world: modern women, with their own purchasing power, looking for professionalism, quality, effectiveness, as well as natural products, with that extra hint of glamour and seduction I have already mentioned.

Asia holds an increasing part in this development, due to the success of these hard-working and ambitious countries. Women there are passionate about cosmetics and quality. I very quickly realised how important this part of the world would be for our business. Except for Japan where the cosmetics industry was already well established, we were among the first brands to arrive on these markets.

In addition to South Korea we rapidly developed our business in Taiwan where we now have a subsidiary. Our subsidiaries in Thailand

and Hong Kong are doing very well. There is also Macao, Singapore, Malaysia and Indonesia. Everywhere, we are sold in the best, and most prestigious department stores.

And of course China is a continent in itself – this immense booming country that has become the world's second biggest economy. We have been working there since the turn of the century, at first through a distributor. Later on, following many trips made by Philippe and Sisley's Asia director, Nicolas Chesnier, we decided to create our own subsidiary so as to invest and manage our development ourselves.

Chinese consumers are passionate. A woman lawyer who loved our brand explained at a launch meeting for Sisleÿa in Beijing that she created a 150-page website about our brand (they were not called blogs at the time) and was closely followed by thousands of consumers! Of course the web came to play a massively important role very early on in China.

With Isabelle and some journalists from the Chinese press.

Our Chinese teams, however, had to cope with particular challenges: the scope of the country and the exceptional growth of the brand. From Beijing and Shanghai in the beginning, we are now present in 42 cities and 120 department stores. These stores have all been modernised and embellished and luxury cosmetics have beautiful counters. New outlets are opening all the time. Our team there has been exceptionally effective and well organised. China, that Philippe regularly visits has today become our leading export market, and employs more people than any other subsidiary.

We have often been asked: are Sisley products the same everywhere?

The answer is Yes. We approach cosmetics more by skin type than by colour, and our range addresses different needs: make-up removal, hydration, anti-aging, sunscreen, body care, etc. It is the cosmetics

Philippe d'Ornano and Nicolas Chesnier, Director of Asia for Sisley, in Thailand, a very promising country like others, with the emergence of a middle class.

culture and consumption patterns that differ. In brief, the world of beauty is both one and many at the same time.

The future of our company is very promising. Sisley has become a major international brand, rooted in the work it has accomplished, our business experience, and its key values which are our family's strength and that of our business, not trying to be like anyone else, always focused on originality, creation and excellence.

For its consumers everywhere, the Sisley brand means a unique notion of quality, refinement, innovation and pleasure of French –and now global – inspiration.

Fair winds, shared and boundless beauty –this is what Isabelle and I wish for Sisley.

The countries where Sisley is present

Andorra
Argentina
Armenia
Aruba
Australia
Austria
Azerbaijan

Bahrain
Belarus
Belgium
Bermuda
Bolivia
Brazil
Bulgaria

Canada
Chile
China
Colombia
Croatia
Curacao
Cyprus
Czech Republic

Denmark
Dubai

Ecuador

Finland
France

Georgia
Germany
Greece

Hungary

India
Indonesia
Ireland
Israel
Italy

Japan

Kazakhstan
Korea
Kuwait

Latvia
Lebanon
Luxembourg

Macedonia
Malaysia
Malta
Mauritius
Mexico
Moldavia
Morocco

Netherlands
New Zealand
Norway

Oman

Panama
Paraguay
Peru
Philippines
Poland
Portugal
Puerto Rico

Qatar

Russia

Saint-Thomas
Serbia
Singapore
Slovakia
Slovenia
Saudi Arabia
South Africa
Spain
Sweden
Switzerland
Syria

Taiwan
Thailand
Tunisia
Turkey

Ukraine
United Kingdom
United States of America
Uruguay
Uzbekistan

Venezuela
Vietnam

Philippe d'Ornano, CEO of Sisley, during a presentation in Taiwan.

Our grandchildren…

Emilio, Shaya, Miléna, Daria, Huberto and Inès;
Alma, Isabelle, Eliya and Luis, summer 2013.

Appendices

Philippe d'Ornano, "To my grandmother"

We all have a name for our grandmother and we called ours affectionately Titine.

And yet she was tall, elegant and could have intimidated us. We knew her life, in pre-war Poland, her three brothers whom she adored. Papa Joseph, his courage and iron will in trying times and in exile.
But she was also affectionate and whimsical, very approachable and close to her grandchildren.
And what more could a small boy wish for than a beautiful, mysterious and adventurous grandmother?
When we were only 7 and 6 years old, she took us on a 1,000 km trip in a little blue Renault which she called her blue bird, to Spain. We didn't cross the Pyrenees on the motorway, but through the Col de Ronceveaux "because it is more beautiful ". While crossing the pass, she repeated in her lovely voice –her slight accent giving the poem a more dramatic tone– *"The Song of Roland"*.
"Come knights let's cross the mountain,
Tremble under our feet deceitful land of Spain."
Needless to say we were fascinated. As we followed the winding road, she explained to us that in bad weather the fog sometimes comes up from the precipice right to the edge of the road and you have to resist the temptation to drive on the white clouds...
We then stopped at Burgos to visit the cathedral. It is there that we discovered Spain.

A grandmother who let us drink beer, which made us so proud, my brother and I.
She told us tales of ghosts and visions, of cupboards that moved, of people lost and found, of the dead visiting the living. As children, we dreamed of seeing ghosts.
A grandmother who was courageous, a fighter, always positive and passionate, she hated injustice and was incapable of fear. She would go out in the street to help a man in danger and drive away his armed assailant. She scolded my aunt and my sister because their car had been stolen at gunpoint and they didn't defend themselves.
A grandmother who called her dog Iago (as in Shakespeare) and fed it crushed fruit because it was healthier. The concoction was delicious for the two weeks we were there, but the dog disappeared one day.
A grandmother at La Renaudière, a proud and sometimes audacious rider. She loved most of all, the country and animals. She used to go on long walks. One day, she came back from her horse ride absolutely delighted: in the middle of the roaring season a beautiful stag had blocked the route and refused to let her past.
A grandmother adored by all of us, who had the simplicity of a true aristocrat. Whenever we went with her to Madrid, all the shopkeepers knew her and greeted her. She took an interest in all of them, and showed real affection.

Titine passed away slowly, perhaps to avoid too bad a shock for those she loved, giving them time to gradually get used to her absence. She taught us a lot as children. For us, she will always remain the fearless cavalier beyond reproach, and the affectionate grandmother of our childhood.

Marc d'Ornano,
Holy Week in Seville, 1983

I arrived in Seville at 5 o'clock, and by 7 I was outside watching the processions. It bored me at first, but I didn't show it. I can't remember the name of the first procession I saw, as I was not very interested. I then went to wait for the Candelaria procession. I spent an hour waiting to see the Christ, then another hour waiting to see the Virgin. It was long and boring, even though two years earlier I took part in it. The procession of other images of Christ and the Virgin lasted for hours.

Then I saw the Candelaria leave the Cathedral. It was late, and despite the crowd I had a good view of everything. Lit by the many candles and dancing to the rhythm of the music, the Virgin was beautiful in the shadows and when she disappeared behind the trees, I felt the need to weave through the crowd to get in front of her, in the first row, and keep up with her. I admired her for a very long time, and when I left, I was sad and would have loved to follow her further. But I had to meet Anna and her friends.

The next day, we went to see the procession of the Virgin of El Baratillo, which began at about 5 o'clock. I met some friends from the previous summer and we took pictures. We arrived too late to see the Christ, but the Virgin was superb. It was still day time and she did not have the mysterious and somewhat sad expression she has at night. She was beautiful, but nothing special. Although all the Virgins are beautiful, some are more so than others for reasons one cannot explain. I didn't find this Virgin as attractive as the one in the procession of The Candelaria or the Virgen de Los Gitanos (The Virgin of the Gypsies). We then watched other processions, but none yielded the exceptional charm of San Bernardo.

We waited for the latter at the bridge it was going to cross. It is surely the most exceptional view you could ever see. Christ, who always goes by first, was crucified, showered with blue, green, red and white spotlights, each colour producing a different expression. The green gave him a deathly pallor, thus conveying great sadness. The red, the same colour as the carnations surrounding him, gave him the look of resurrection. The bearers made Christ dance to music for a good hundred metres. The spotlights on him threw a shadow of his crucified body on the wall behind, creating a real yet mysterious sensation. It was the last procession of Holy Wednesday that I can remember in detail, as opposed to the others.

The next day, Holy Thursday, was the longest day. After attending the Holy Thursday mass at 5:30, we stayed outside the whole night watching the processions. The first was the Quinta Angustia, in which two of my friends, José and Eduardo were taking part. Christ and the Virgin were together and not separated as they are most of the time. As Christ died on Good Friday, there is no music accompanying the processions. It shows two men on ladders taking the dead body of Christ down from the cross under the sad pitying gaze of the Holy Virgin, Saint John and Mary Magdalene. This

Christ, beautiful as it was, didn't touch me as much as the others, no doubt because I had already seen him during the day, without the sorrowful and mysterious atmosphere at night, only lit by the candles.

After the Quinta Angustia, on Good Friday, at 1:30 a.m., we went to see the Cristo del Silencio. We waited over an hour, but it didn't seem long as we were talking at the time. As its name indicates, Christ finally appears in complete silence, without any music, surrounded only by the respect of the vast crowd waiting for him. There is not a single sound, except far away. I was very moved. His face didn't seem to have suffered physically, but more so mentally as, at the moment of his death when he raised his eyes to heaven and said, "Father forgive them, for they know not what they do." I have never felt as I did with the Cristo del Cachorro (Christ of Expiration). The Cristo del Silencio is the only one to carry the cross upside down and "the Nazarenos", the penitents who accompany the procession carry a cross the same way. We only saw it leave the church, but the overwhelming silence made me think about how much Christ suffered.

After watching various processions, we went to watch the Virgen de los Gitanos. It was the most memorable. She was beautiful and danced continuously down the narrow streets through which she passed and turned to salute the Convent of Angela de la Cruz. We followed her for a long time. We were right at the front and I remember how moved I was looking at her. She seemed alive, more beautiful than ever, with an unbelievable charm. The music was the same as for the Candelaria, very joyous and compelling. All the people who joined this procession were gypsies, which gave this tanned-skin Virgin a distinctive personality.

The Cristo del Grand Poder, which we saw next, was one of the most touching and impressive. There was no way of getting near as the discipline here is much stricter. It moved very fast, with no music or dancing, and the silence of the people while it passed was as impressive as for the Cristo del Silencio. The people carrying him gave it the impression he was actually marching, particularly when watching Christ arrive from a distance, with his floating tunic, a characteristic impression unlike any other. We had waited several hours to see it for only a few minutes or even seconds, as it moved very fast. While it was passing, I was struck by the sense of contemplation, totally exceptional. People don't come to see the Cristo del Grand Poder as tourists, but to pray. Christ is bent over by the weight of the cross and he really seems to be suffering. His hands and his face are deformed by pain. You can see his veins and you get the impression that they're going to burst at any time.

After waiting the entire Holy Week to see her, at around 7:30 in the morning La Macarena finally arrived in the distance. I was with Marta, Ana Parias and Maria José, who knew people living in a house which overlooked the procession. From there we saw her coming behind men dressed like Roman soldiers and we left the house to follow her for a few minutes. She is undoubtedly different from the others. Once again in the front row, I was able to admire the expression on her face that no other Virgin had. Her two famous tears, her emaciated face showing the suffering she had felt and, despite that, joyous music making her dance practically every ten meters. A massive crowd had come to admire and follow her. The candles were all gone, as she had come out many hours earlier. Although I saw La Macarena during the day, I found her superb and her sadness only gave her more charm.

Finally there came the Esperanza de Triana. I say finally, because Maria José talked to me about her all week, saying she was the most beautiful of them all. It was roughly 8:30 in the morning when she arrived. She was dressed in green and looked superb. I must admit that I was expecting beauty and expressiveness, if not superior at least comparable to La Macarena. Unfortunately, I didn't find any such charm in this Virgin, although I watched her for a long time. She was coloured and appeared very adult, which removed some of the charming purity of La Macarena. And sadness wasn't as evident on her face as in the others. It is with this Virgin that we ended a very moving night.

On Good Friday, we watched other processions, but only two of them were memorable. The first was that of the Cachorro, which we saw leave the church. We were inside and Christ was heavily marked by physical suffering evident on his face. He was crucified, knees bloody, ribs sticking out from his sunken chest, arms stretched out with veins straining, and with all that, his eyes turned to heaven with great pity. This Christ is also called the Cristo de La Expiracion (of Expiration), a name that fits it perfectly, as you sense he is going to die any moment. The Virgin is also very beautiful, but I don't remember her as well, as the image of Christ was particularly powerful.

The last procession I watched that Friday was the Virgin of the "O", which for me concluded Holy Week. I waited for her inside the church of the Virgin of the Esperanza de Triana, which allowed me to contemplate the latter once again. I wasn't very close to Christ or to the Virgin of the "O", which made it difficult to see their expression in detail, even though the spectacle was very beautiful. Christ arrived in front of the church and began dancing and turning to face the Esperanza de Triana. He saluted her for a few minutes, dancing. The Virgin of the "O" did the same after Christ, but she didn't turn like he had, probably because she was late. The performance was superb and very colourful.

I have tried, through these various scenes, to put down on paper what I felt during that Holy Week.

I believe I can sum it all up by: "Yes, Seville offers the mystery of Christ who died for Love. He progresses, street after street, corner after corner, accompanied by the Holy Virgin who shares his pain."

The Sevillan Parias family,
Marquis of Monte Florido, where Marc stayed during Holy Week,
sent us after his death this text written by him–
he was 17 years old when he wrote it.

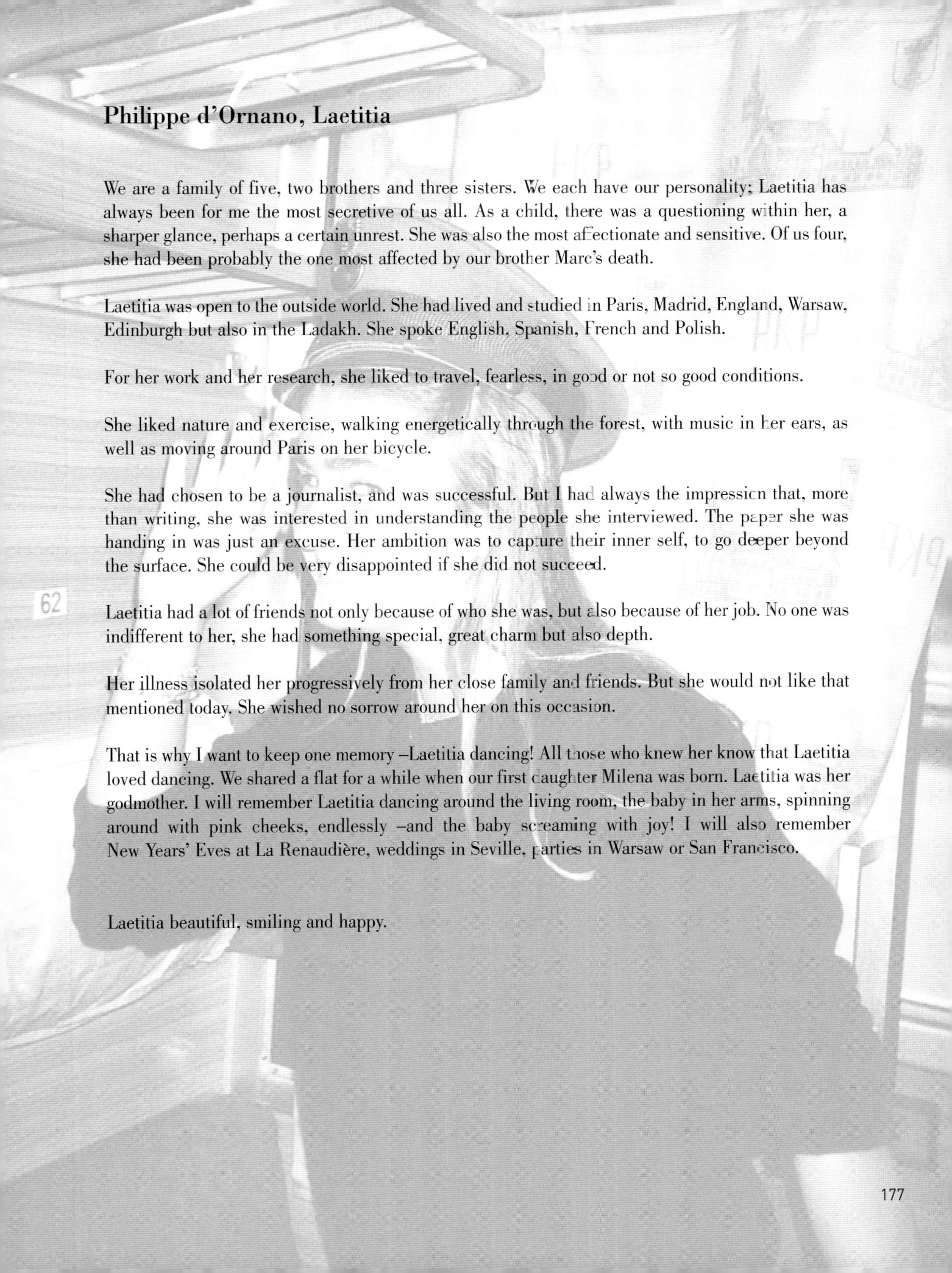

Philippe d'Ornano, Laetitia

We are a family of five, two brothers and three sisters. We each have our personality; Laetitia has always been for me the most secretive of us all. As a child, there was a questioning within her, a sharper glance, perhaps a certain unrest. She was also the most affectionate and sensitive. Of us four, she had been probably the one most affected by our brother Marc's death.

Laetitia was open to the outside world. She had lived and studied in Paris, Madrid, England, Warsaw, Edinburgh but also in the Ladakh. She spoke English, Spanish, French and Polish.

For her work and her research, she liked to travel, fearless, in good or not so good conditions.

She liked nature and exercise, walking energetically through the forest, with music in her ears, as well as moving around Paris on her bicycle.

She had chosen to be a journalist, and was successful. But I had always the impression that, more than writing, she was interested in understanding the people she interviewed. The paper she was handing in was just an excuse. Her ambition was to capture their inner self, to go deeper beyond the surface. She could be very disappointed if she did not succeed.

Laetitia had a lot of friends not only because of who she was, but also because of her job. No one was indifferent to her, she had something special, great charm but also depth.

Her illness isolated her progressively from her close family and friends. But she would not like that mentioned today. She wished no sorrow around her on this occasion.

That is why I want to keep one memory –Laetitia dancing! All those who knew her know that Laetitia loved dancing. We shared a flat for a while when our first daughter Milena was born. Laetitia was her godmother. I will remember Laetitia dancing around the living room, the baby in her arms, spinning around with pink cheeks, endlessly –and the baby screaming with joy! I will also remember New Years' Eves at La Renaudière, weddings in Seville, parties in Warsaw or San Francisco.

Laetitia beautiful, smiling and happy.

A brief chronology

March 31st 1926
Hubert d'Ornano is born, son of Guillaume and Élisabeth d'Ornano, née Michalska, in Melgiew (Poland).

1934
Hubert d'Ornano returns to France.

1935
Armand Petitjean and Guillaume d'Ornano create Lancôme.

1946
Michel and Hubert d'Ornano found the company Jean d'Albret.

1953
Guillaume, Michel and Hubert d'Ornano launch Orlane.

1963
Hubert marries Isabelle d'Ornano, née Potocka, a union that would produce five children: Philippe (1964), Marc (1966-1986), Elisabeth (1968), Marie-Laetitia (1970-2013) and Christine (1973).

1968
The company Jean d'Albret-Orlane is sold following the entry into politics of Michel d'Ornano, Mayor of Deauville and Member of French Parliament, President of the General Council of Calvados, then of the Regional Council of Basse-Normandie, several times minister.

1971
Hubert d'Ornano becomes Chairman and CEO (until 1975) of Jean d'Albret-Orlane and its subsidiary Jean-Louis Scherrer.

1976
Hubert d'Ornano takes over Sisley, a company specializing in phyto-cosmetology.

1977
Sisley proposes a complete range of skincare products, make-up and perfumes, including the perfume Eau de Campagne.

1980
Émulsion Ecologique.

1986
Philippe d'Ornano joins Sisley.

1989
Crème Réparatrice au Beurre de Karité. Complexe Séro-Botanique Activateur de Nuit.

1990
Super Crème Solaire Visage.
Eau du Soir perfume.
First international subsidiary in Germany.

1997
Christine d'Ornano joins Sisley.

1999
Sisleÿa Global Anti-âge is launched after ten years of development.

2003
Acquisition and development of the Francos Production Centre in Blois, on the Loire river.

2005
All Day All Year.

2006
Sisleÿa Réducteur Rides Quotidien.
Sunleÿa, sun cream and anti-age after-sun.
Soir de Lune perfume.

2007
Hydro-Global intense moisturizer.
Sisley-d'Ornano Foundation created under the aegis of the Fondation de France.

2009
Supremÿa night cream.
Sunleÿa anti-age after-sun.
Les Eaux de Sisley.

2011
Saint-Ouen-L'Aumône Research Centre built by Sisley opens northwest of Paris.
Sisleÿum, global care for men.
Eau d'Ikar perfume.

2012
Masque Crème à la Rose Noire.

2013
Philippe d'Ornano becomes Chairman and CEO of Sisley.
Christine d'Ornano is Senior Vice President.

2014
Eau tropicale perfume.

Photographic credits

David Atlan: pp. 81 and 150.

Private collection: pp. 13, 15, 128, 127 and 130-131.
Oleg Covian: p. 170 and dust jacket.

Olivier Dassault: pp. 80 and 155.

Église Notre-Dame de l'Assomption: p. 165.

Le Figaro: p. 103.
Martine Franck: pp. 79 and 122 (top left),

Horst P. Horst: p. 139 (top).

Bronislaw Krzysztof: pp. 117 (left) and 161.

Véronique Landry: p. 124.
Guillaume de Laubier: p. 166-167.
Philippe Ledru: p. 72.
Bertrand Leroy (reproduced by): pp. 41, 61, 63, 68, 69, 85 (top middle), 94, 112, 128 and 143 (bottom).

Ricardo Macarron: p. 83.
Guy Marineau: p. 138.
Musée national des Invalides / RMN: pp. 12, 30, 33, 38 and 40 (painting by Jean-Baptiste-Edouard Detaille).

Louis Pilmann: p. 125.

Famille d'Ornano: pp. 6, 9, 10, 11, 17, 19, 23, 25, 41, 43, 45, 50, 51, 52, 53, 55, 56, 57, 58, 60, 61, 63, 64, 66, 68, 69, 70, 73, 84-85, 86-87, 89, 90-91, 122-123, 124, 127, 130-131, 133, 134, 135, 139 (bottom), 141, 142, 147, 149, 152 (right), 171, 172, 177 and 181.
Philippe d'Ornano: p. 140.

Paris-Turf: 143 (bottom).

All Rights Reserved: pp. 4, 8, 24, 26, 29, 32, 44, 46, 49, 52-53 (bottom), 75, 76, 88-89 (bottom), 93, 94, 95, 98, 143, 171 and 174.

Sisley: pp. 100, 104-105, 106, 111, 112, 116-117, 121, 137, 145, 146, 151, 157, 158, 160-161, 162, 166-167, 168 and 169.

Thomson Newspapers (All Rights Reserved): photograph of the picture on the front cover, pp. 63, 67 and 74.

Hubert de Watrigant: p. 142 (bottom).

With Christine in 1990, when I still smoked cigars…!

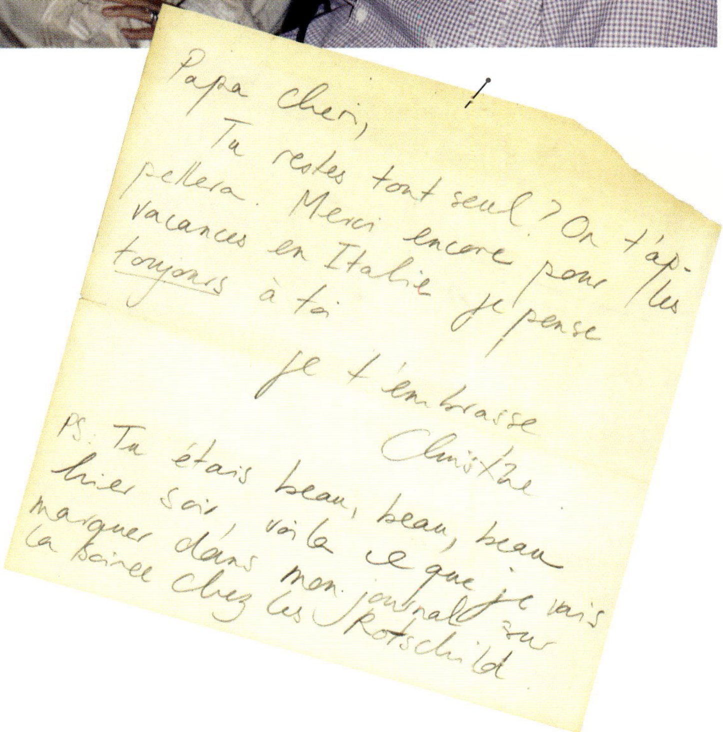

Papa Chéri,
Tu restes tout seul? On t'ap-
pellera. Merci encore pour les
vacances en Italie je pense
toujours à toi

Je t'embrasse
Christine

PS: Tu étais beau, beau, beau
hier soir, voilà ce que je vais
marquer dans mon journal sur
la soirée chez les Rotschild

Acknowledgments

First of all I want to thank Isabelle without whom none of this would have been possible, this book and its English version *Boundless Beauty* would not exist.

My thanks go also to the members of the teams at Sisley, past and present, who have contributed from the beginning through their work and their capacities to promote with us the development and success of the superb brand that Sisley has become. I cannot list everyone individually, but all of you remain important in my eyes.

Likewise everyone who has helped Isabelle and me produce this book by reviewing it and sharing their memories and their points of view.

My children, Philippe, Elisabeth and Christine; Anne d'Ornano, who shared her memories of Michel with us; Pierre Potocki and Dosia Potocka, Isabelle's brother and sister;

Jean Chalon and Stanislas Dwernicki for their precious advice and careful readings.

At Sisley, Gisèle Bidaud, Philippe Lacassagne, Véronique Landry, André Reich, Roger Renou, Philippe Valentin, as well as Francette Léguillon and my faithful assistants, Nicole Lecomte, Andrée Giroud and Joanna Bonis; at La Renaudière, Claude Liégeois and Philippe Coutant.

Thanks also to Cerith Gardiner for giving her additional English touch to the text.

And of course my thanks go to Félix Torres, who helped us establish and edit this text through his understanding and capacity to capture the spirit of the d'Ornano family and that of Sisley.